100
Chinese Dishes

100
Chinese Dishes

Edited by
Maureen Callis

octopus

Contents

Introduction 5
Soups 6
Fish Dishes 10
Poultry Dishes 18
Meat Dishes 30
Vegetable & Salad Dishes 50
Desserts 58
Special Chinese Ingredients 62
Index 63

NOTES

Standard spoon measurements are used in all recipes
1 tablespoon = one 15 ml spoon
1 teaspoon = one 5 ml spoon
All spoon measures are level.

For all recipes, quantities are given in metric, imperial and American measures.
Follow one set of measures only because they are not interchangeable.

First published 1982 by
Octopus Books Limited
59 Grosvenor Street, London W1

© 1982 Octopus Books Limited

ISBN 0 7064 1766 6

Produced by Mandarin Publishers Ltd
22a Westlands Rd
Quarry Bay, Hong Kong
Printed in Hong Kong

These recipes have previously appeared in The Complete
Encyclopedia of Chinese Cooking and The Encyclopedia of
Asian Cooking both published by Octopus Books Limited.

Introduction

Chinese cooking has a tradition that goes back thousands of years. Over the past twenty years this tradition has spread across the world and the pleasures of Chinese food are now more widely available to us all.

But there is still an air of mystery surrounding this ancient cuisine and a belief that it is difficult to "cook Chinese". This book aims to show that this is just not so — once you have learnt a few basic principles, authentic Chinese food can be cooked with ease. No special equipment is necessary and the cooking methods are much the same as ours. The main differences lie in the preparation of foods and the use of flavourings.

Food Preparation
As a large number of dishes are cooked quickly, the ingredients must be cut into very small pieces of equal size. The various methods of cutting are —

Slicing: cut the food into paper-thin slices the size of a stamp. Cut meat across grain; vegetables on slant.

Shredding: slice the food as above, then place the slices on top of each other and cut into matchstick strips.

Dicing: cut into 1 cm/$\frac{1}{2}$ inch wide and thick strips, then cut across at 1 cm/$\frac{1}{2}$ inch intervals to give cubes.

Diagonal cutting: this is used for vegetables like celery and carrots. Make a diagonal cut straight down, then half turn and slice diagonally again, giving a diamond shape.

Cooking Methods
The most important factor in Chinese cooking is the degree of heat which governs the cooking time. It is therefore difficult to give precise cooking times as much depends on the type of utensils used and the size of the ingredients. The times given in the recipes are therefore only a guide. The main cooking methods are simply explained and easily followed.

Clear simmering is a slow process where the food is cooked in clear broth or water and, by keeping the temperature very low, the liquid stays clear. Meat and poultry cooked this way are tender enough to be pulled apart with chopsticks. They are usually served with dips to add flavour. The broth is flavoured by adding dried or pickled ingredients at the start of the cooking and fresh vegetables at the end. Serve as a soup with the vegetables, which should be crisp.

Quick steaming is best reserved for very fresh foods, especially fish. The food is first seasoned or marinated then steamed vigorously over high heat for a short time.

Red-cooking is a form of stewing with soy sauce. The soy sauce imparts a rich flavour and reddish-brown colour. Most meat can be cooked this way.

Quick roasting (Cha Shao) can only be used on good quality, tender meat. The meat is first marinated then roasted at a high temperature for a short time.

Stir-frying is the method most commonly used in China. Heat the pan over high heat, add a little oil or lard until smoking, then add the ingredients and toss and stir constantly for a short time. The food should be crisp so do not overcook or it will burn or become soggy.

Cooking Equipment
You can cook any Chinese dish using everyday pans, although you may like to have the two basic Chinese utensils. Both are readily obtainable and reasonably priced.

The Wok is cone-shaped with a rounded bottom, usually made of iron. It maintains an intense steady heat, the shape enabling the heat to spread evenly so only a short cooking time is required. A deep, heavy frying pan makes a reasonable substitute.

Bamboo Steamers stack on top of each other, enabling four or five dishes to be steamed at once. A traditional steamer or double boiler can also be used. If you don't have one of these, place the food on a heatproof plate on a rack 5 cm/2 inches above the water in a large pan.

Serving Chinese Food
Harmony is the most important point to consider when planning a menu. Choose dishes which complement each other, but contrast in flavour, texture and colour.

As a general guide, serve one main dish per person and one soup. Thus a dinner for two would consist of two main dishes and one soup; a dinner for six would comprise five or six main dishes and one soup. A vegetable dish can be served instead of or as well as the soup. The more people eating, the more variety there should be: don't just increase the amount of food, increase the number of dishes.

The serving suggestions in this book are intended only as a general guide, based on the principle above.

This selection of recipes is made up of simple dishes that have become familiar and popular in the West, plus a few lesser-known ones for the more adventurous to try. (Information on special Chinese ingredients is given on page 62 with some suggestions for substitutes for those who have difficulty in obtaining the Chinese ingredients.)

Soups

Beef and Egg-Flower Soup

METRIC/IMPERIAL	AMERICAN
1.2 litres/2 pints chicken stock or water	5 cups chicken stock or water
100 g/4 oz beef steak, coarsely chopped	½ cup coarsely chopped round steak
2 teaspoons salt	2 teaspoons salt
1 celery stick, chopped	1 celery stalk, chopped
1 egg, beaten	1 egg, beaten
freshly ground black pepper	freshly ground black pepper
few spring onions, sliced, to garnish	few scallions, sliced, for garnish

Bring the stock or water to the boil in a pan, then add the beef, salt and celery. Bring back to the boil, then add the egg, a little at a time, stirring vigorously to achieve the 'egg-flower' effect. Add pepper to taste.

Pour into a warmed soup tureen and sprinkle with spring onions (scallions). Serve hot.
Serves 4 to 6

Pork Spareribs Soup

METRIC/IMPERIAL	AMERICAN
450 g/1 lb pork spareribs	1 lb pork spareribs
50 g/2 oz lard	¼ cup lard
2 teaspoons salt	2 teaspoons salt
4 slices root ginger	4 slices ginger root
1.5 litres/2½ pints water	6¼ cups water
2 spring onions, chopped	2 scallions, chopped
pinch of monosodium glutamate (optional)	pinch of msg (optional)

Beef and Egg-Flower Soup (above)
Pork and Tomato Soup (below)

Cut the spareribs into 2.5 cm/1 inch pieces. Melt the lard in a large pan. Add the spareribs and fry for about 10 minutes. Add the salt, ginger and water and bring to the boil. Simmer for 2 hours.

Add the spring onions (scallions) and mono-sodium glutamate (msg) and cook, stirring, for 2 to 3 minutes. Serve hot.
Serves 4

Pork and Tomato Soup

METRIC/IMPERIAL	AMERICAN
100 g/4 oz boned lean pork, very thinly sliced	½ cup very thinly sliced boneless pork
1 teaspoon soy sauce	1 teaspoon soy sauce
1 teaspoon dry sherry	1 teaspoon pale dry sherry
2 tablespoons oil	2 tablespoons oil
1 small onion, chopped	1 small onion, chopped
2 tomatoes, chopped	2 tomatoes, chopped
1.2 litres/2 pints chicken stock	5 cups chicken stock
2 teaspoons salt	2 teaspoons salt
freshly ground black pepper	freshly ground black pepper
1 egg, beaten	1 egg, beaten
chopped coriander leaves or parsley to garnish	chopped coriander leaves or parsley for garnish

Put the pork in a bowl with the soy sauce and sherry. Stir well and leave to marinate for about 20 minutes.

Heat the oil in a wok or deep pan, add the onion and pork and stir-fry for 2 minutes. Add the tomatoes and stock and bring to the boil. Add the salt with pepper to taste and simmer for a few minutes.

Stir in the egg, then immediately pour into a warmed soup tureen and sprinkle with coriander or parsley. Serve hot.
Serves 4 to 6

Duck and Cabbage Soup

METRIC/IMPERIAL	AMERICAN
1 duck carcass, with giblets	1 duck carcass, with giblets
2 slices root ginger	2 slices ginger root
450 g/1 lb Chinese cabbage, sliced	1 lb bok choy, sliced
salt	salt
freshly ground black pepper	freshly ground black pepper

Break up the carcass and place in a large pan. Add the giblets and any other meat left over from the duck.

Cover with water, add the ginger and bring to the boil. Skim, then lower the heat and simmer for at least 30 minutes.

Add the cabbage (boy choy) and salt and pepper to taste. Continue cooking for about 20 minutes.

Discard the duck carcass and ginger slices and check the seasoning. Pour the soup into a warmed soup tureen. Serve hot.

Serves 4 to 6

Corn Soup

METRIC/IMPERIAL	AMERICAN
1.2 litres/2 pints stock	5 cups stock
1 × 425 g/15 oz can cream-style sweetcorn	1 × 15 oz can cream-style corn
1 teaspoon salt	1 teaspoon salt
1 tablespoon dry sherry	1 tablespoon pale dry sherry
freshly ground black pepper	freshly ground black pepper
2 tablespoons cornflour, blended with 2 tablespoons water	2 tablespoons cornstarch, blended with 2 tablespoons water
2 eggs, beaten	2 eggs, beaten
1–2 spring onions, chopped	1–2 scallions, chopped

Bring the stock to the boil in a saucepan. Stir in the corn, then add the salt, sherry and pepper to taste. Add the blended cornflour (cornstarch) and simmer, stirring constantly, until thickened.

Lower the heat and add the beaten eggs in a thin stream, stirring constantly; the soup should not be boiling when the eggs are added. Pour into a warmed soup tureen and sprinkle with the spring onion (scallion). Serve hot.

Serves 4 to 6

Chicken and Mushroom Soup

METRIC/IMPERIAL	AMERICAN
25 g/1 oz Chinese dried mushrooms	8 medium Chinese dried mushrooms
1 chicken, weighing 1 kg/2–2¼ lb	1 chicken, weighing 2–2¼ lb
1 tablespoon dry sherry	1 tablespoon pale dry sherry
1 spring onion	1 scallion
1 slice root ginger	1 slice ginger root
1½ teaspoons salt	1½ teaspoons salt

Soak the mushrooms in warm water for 20 minutes. Drain and squeeze dry, reserving the soaking liquid. Discard the mushroom stalks.

Put the chicken in a large pan of boiling water. Boil rapidly for 2 to 3 minutes, then remove the chicken and rinse thoroughly under cold running water.

Put the chicken and mushrooms in a pan or flame-proof casserole with a tight-fitting lid. Add just enough water to cover the chicken, then add the sherry, spring onion (scallion), ginger and reserved mushroom liquid. Bring to the boil, then cover and simmer for at least 2 hours.

Just before serving, skim the surface of the soup; discard the spring onion (scallion) and ginger if wished. Stir in the salt. Lift the chicken into a warmed soup tureen then pour in the soup. Serve hot.

Serves 4 to 6

Note: As the chicken is served whole in its cooking liquid, this soup can be served as a complete meal. The meat should be very tender so that it can easily be torn into pieces with chopsticks or a soup spoon.

Chicken and Noodle Soup

METRIC/IMPERIAL	AMERICAN
pinch of salt	pinch of salt
1 egg white	1 egg white
1 teaspoon cornflour	1 teaspoon cornstarch
225 g/8 oz chicken breast meat, shredded	1 cup shredded chicken breast meat
350 g/12 oz egg noodles	$\frac{3}{4}$ lb egg noodles
1.2 litres/2 pints chicken stock	5 cups chicken stock
40 g/1$\frac{1}{2}$ oz lard	3 tablespoons lard
100 g/4 oz canned bamboo shoot, drained and shredded	1 cup shredded canned bamboo shoot
50 g/2 oz mushrooms, shredded	$\frac{1}{2}$ cup shredded mushrooms
225 g/8 oz spinach	$\frac{1}{2}$ lb spinach
2–3 spring onions, cut into 2.5 cm/1 inch pieces	2–3 scallions, cut into 1 inch pieces
Sauce:	**Sauce:**
3 tablespoons soy sauce	3 tablespoons soy sauce
1 tablespoon dry sherry	1 tablespoon pale dry sherry
1 teaspoon salt	1 teaspoon salt
1 teaspoon sugar	1 teaspoon sugar
1 teaspoon sesame seed oil	1 teaspoon sugar
	1 teaspoon sesame seed oil

Mix together the salt, egg white and cornflour (cornstarch) in a bowl. Add the chicken and turn to coat thoroughly.

Cook the noodles in boiling water for about 5 minutes or until tender. Drain and place in a warmed soup tureen. Bring the chicken stock to the boil and pour over the noodles. Keep hot.

Melt the lard in a wok or frying pan (skillet). Add the chicken, bamboo shoot, mushrooms, spinach and spring onions (scallions) and stir-fry for 2 minutes.

Combine the sauce ingredients and stir into the pan. When the liquid starts to bubble, pour it over the noodles and stock mixture and serve at once.
Serves 6

Shredded Pork and Noodles in Soup

METRIC/IMPERIAL	AMERICAN
3–4 Chinese dried mushrooms	3–4 Chinese dried mushrooms
225 g/8 oz boned lean pork, shredded	1 cup shredded pork loin
1 tablespoon soy sauce	1 tablespoon soy sauce
1 tablespoon dry sherry	1 tablespoon pale dry sherry
1 teaspoon sugar	1 teaspoon sugar
2 teaspoons cornflour	2 teaspoons cornstarch
350 g/12 oz egg noodles	$\frac{3}{4}$ lb egg noodles
3 tablespoons vegetable oil	3 tablespoons vegetable oil
2 spring onions, cut into 2.5 cm/1 inch lengths	2 scallions, cut into 1 inch lengths
100 g/4 oz canned bamboo shoot, drained and shredded	1 cup shredded canned bamboo shoot
salt	salt
600 ml/1 pint boiling chicken stock	2$\frac{1}{2}$ cups boiling chicken stock

Soak the mushrooms in warm water for 20 minutes. Drain and squeeze dry, reserving the soaking liquid. Discard the hard stalks, then thinly slice the caps.

Put the pork in a bowl with the soy sauce, sherry, sugar and cornflour (cornstarch). Stir well and leave to marinate for about 20 minutes.

Cook the noodles in boiling water for about 5 minutes; drain.

Heat half the oil in a wok or frying pan (skillet), add the pork and stir-fry for 2 minutes. Remove from the pan with a slotted spoon and drain on kitchen paper towels.

Heat the remaining oil in the pan, add the spring onions (scallions), mushrooms and bamboo shoot. Stir and add a little salt. Return the pork to the pan, together with the mushroom liquid, and heat through.

Place the noodles in a warmed soup tureen, pour over the boiling stock then add the pork and vegetables. Serve hot.
Serves 4 to 6

Fish Dishes

Crab Omelet

METRIC/IMPERIAL	AMERICAN
2 spring onions	2 scallions
4 eggs, beaten	4 eggs, beaten
salt	salt
3 tablespoons vegetable oil	3 tablespoons vegetable oil
2 slices root ginger, shredded	2 slices ginger root, shredded
175 g/6 oz fresh, frozen or canned crabmeat	6 oz fresh, frozen or canned crabmeat
1 tablespoon dry sherry	1 tablespoon pale dry sherry
1½ tablespoons soy sauce	1½ tablespoons soy sauce
2 teaspoons sugar	2 teaspoons sugar
Garnish:	**Garnish:**
shredded lettuce	shredded lettuce
tomato and grape (optional)	tomato and grape (optional)

Cut the white part of the spring onions (scallions) into 2.5 cm/1 inch lengths. Chop the green parts finely and beat into the eggs, with salt to taste.

Heat the oil in a wok or frying pan (skillet). Add the white spring onions (scallions), ginger, crab and sherry. Stir-fry for a few seconds then add the soy sauce and sugar. Lower the heat, pour in the egg mixture and cook for 30 seconds.

Transfer to a warmed serving dish and garnish with shredded lettuce. To finish, place a serrated-cut tomato half and a grape in the centre to resemble a flower head, if liked. Serve immediately.
Serves 2

Stir-Fried Squid with Mixed Vegetables

METRIC/IMPERIAL	AMERICAN
450 g/1 lb squid	1 lb squid
2 slices root ginger, finely chopped	2 slices ginger root, finely chopped
1 tablespoon dry sherry	1 tablespoon pale dry sherry
1 tablespoon cornflour	1 tablespoon cornstarch
15 g/½ oz dried wood ears	½ cup dried tree ears
4 tablespoons vegetable oil	¼ cup vegetable oil
2 spring onions, white part only, cut into 2.5 cm/1 inch lengths	2 scallions, white part only, cut into 1 inch lengths
225 g/8 oz cauliflower or broccoli, divided into florets	½ lb cauliflower or broccoli, divided into florets
2 carrots, cut into diamond-shaped chunks	2 carrots, cut into diamond-shaped chunks
1 teaspoon salt	1 teaspoon salt
1 teaspoon sugar	1 teaspoon sugar
1 teaspoon sesame seed oil	1 teaspoon sesame seed oil

Clean the squid, discarding the head, transparent backbone and ink bag. Cut the flesh into thin slices or rings. Place in a bowl with half the ginger, the sherry and cornflour (cornstarch). Mix well and leave to marinate for about 20 minutes.

Soak the wood (tree) ears in warm water for 20 minutes. Drain and break into small pieces, discarding the hard bits.

Heat 2 tablespoons of the oil in a wok or frying pan (skillet). Add the spring onions (scallions), cauliflower or broccoli, carrots, wood (tree) ears and remaining ginger. Stir, then add the salt and sugar and continue cooking until the vegetables are tender, adding a little water if necessary. Remove from the pan with a slotted spoon and drain.

Heat the remaining oil in the pan, add the squid and stir-fry for about 1 minute; do not overcook or it will be tough and chewy. Return the vegetables to the pan, add the sesame seed oil and mix all the ingredients well together. Serve hot.
Serves 4

Stir-Fried Squid with Mixed Vegetables (above)
Crab Omelet (below)

Stir-Fried Prawns (Shrimp) and Peas

METRIC/IMPERIAL	AMERICAN
450 g/1 lb peeled prawns	1 lb shelled shrimp
1 egg white	1 egg white
2 teaspoons cornflour	2 teaspoons cornstarch
3 tablespoons vegetable oil	3 tablespoons vegetable oil
2 spring onions, white part only, finely chopped	2 scallions, white part only, finely chopped
1 slice root ginger, finely chopped	1 slice ginger root, finely chopped
225 g/8 oz fresh or frozen and thawed peas	1½ cups fresh or frozen and thawed peas
1 teaspoon salt	1 teaspoon salt
1 tablespoon dry sherry	1 tablespoon pale dry sherry

Put the prawns (shrimp) in a bowl with the egg white and cornflour (cornstarch). Mix well and leave to marinate for about 20 minutes.

Heat the oil in a wok or frying pan (skillet), add the prawns (shrimp) and stir-fry for about 1 minute. Remove from the pan with a slotted spoon and drain on kitchen paper towels.

Increase the heat, add the spring onions (scallions), ginger, peas and salt and stir-fry for 2 minutes if using fresh peas, 1 minute if using frozen.

Return the prawns (shrimp) to the pan, add the sherry and cook for 1 minute. Serve hot.
Serves 4

Crispy-Skin Fish

METRIC/IMPERIAL	AMERICAN
750 g/1½ lb small fish (whiting, herring, small trout, etc)	1½ lb small fish (whiting, herring, small trout, etc)
3–4 slices root ginger, chopped	3–4 slices ginger root, chopped
1 tablespoon salt	1 tablespoon salt
1½ tablespoons plain flour	1½ tablespoons all-purpose flour
oil for deep-frying	oil for deep-frying
parsley sprigs to garnish	parsley sprigs for garnish

Slit the fish along the belly, clean and rinse thoroughly; leave the heads and tails intact.

Rub the fish inside and out with the ginger and salt. Leave for 3 hours. Rub with the flour and leave for 30 minutes.

Heat the oil in a wok or deep-fryer to 180°C/350°F. Deep-fry the fish in batches for 3 to 4 minutes, or until they are crisp and golden brown. Drain the fish on kitchen paper towels and keep hot while frying the remaining fish.

Return them all to the oil and fry for 2½ to 3 minutes, or until very crisp. Serve hot, garnished with a few parsley sprigs.
Serves 4

Prawn (Shrimp) Balls with Broccoli

METRIC/IMPERIAL	AMERICAN
225 g/8 oz Dublin Bay or Pacific prawns in shell	½ lb unshelled jumbo shrimp
1 slice root ginger, finely chopped	1 slice ginger root, finely chopped
1 teaspoon dry sherry	1 teaspoon pale dry sherry
1 egg white	1 egg white
1 tablespoon cornflour	1 tablespoon cornstarch
3 tablespoons vegetable oil	3 tablespoons vegetable oil
2 spring onions, finely chopped	2 scallions, finely chopped
225 g/8 oz broccoli, cut into small pieces	½ lb broccoli, cut into small pieces
1 teaspoon salt	1 teaspoon salt
1 teaspoon sugar	1 teaspoon sugar

Wash the unshelled prawns (shrimp) and dry thoroughly with kitchen paper towels. Using a sharp knife, make a shallow incision down the back of the prawn (shrimp) and pull out the black intestinal vein. Split each prawn (shrimp) in half lengthways, then cut into small pieces so that they will become little round balls when cooked.

Put the prawns (shrimp) in a bowl with the ginger, sherry, egg white and cornflour (cornstarch). Stir well and leave to marinate for about 20 minutes.

Heat 1 tablespoon of the oil in a wok or frying pan (skillet), add the prawns (shrimp) and stir-fry for about 5 minutes, or until they turn pink; do not overcook or they will lose their delicate flavour. Remove from the pan with a slotted spoon and set aside.

Heat the remaining oil in the pan, add the spring onions (scallions) and broccoli, stir, then add the salt and sugar. Cook until the broccoli is just tender, then add the prawns (shrimp) and stir well. Serve hot.
Serves 4

Soy-Braised Cod or Halibut

METRIC/IMPERIAL	AMERICAN
50 g/2 oz lard	$\frac{1}{4}$ cup lard
3–4 spring onions, finely chopped	3–4 scallions, finely chopped
2–3 slices root ginger, finely chopped	2–3 slices ginger root, finely chopped
450 g/1 lb cod or halibut fillets, quartered	1 lb cod or halibut fillets, quartered
2 tablespoons dry sherry	2 tablespoons pale dry sherry
2 tablespoons soy sauce	2 tablespoons soy sauce
1 tablespoon sugar	1 tablespoon sugar
120 ml/4 fl oz water	$\frac{1}{2}$ cup water
1 tablespoon cornflour, blended with 1$\frac{1}{2}$ tablespoons water	1 tablespoon cornstarch, blended with 1$\frac{1}{2}$ tablespoons water
1 teaspoon sesame seed oil	1 teaspoon sesame seed oil
shredded spring onion to garnish	shredded scallion for garnish

Melt the lard in a wok or frying pan (skillet) over high heat. Add the spring onions (scallions) and ginger and stir-fry for a few seconds. Add the fish pieces and stir very gently to separate. Add the sherry and bring to the boil, then stir in the soy sauce, sugar and water. Simmer for about 10 minutes.

Add the blended cornflour (cornstarch) and simmer, stirring, until thickened, then add the sesame seed oil. Garnish with the shredded spring onion (scallion) and serve.
Serves 4

Fish Slices in White Sauce

METRIC/IMPERIAL	AMERICAN
1 egg white	1 egg white
1 teaspoon salt	1 teaspoon salt
1 tablespoon cornflour	1 tablespoon cornstarch
450 g/1 lb plaice or sole fillets, cut into small pieces	1 lb flounder or sole fillets, cut into small pieces
3 tablespoons vegetable oil	3 tablespoons vegetable oil
2 spring onions, finely chopped	2 scallions, finely chopped
1 garlic clove, finely chopped	1 garlic clove, finely chopped
2 tablespoons dry sherry	2 tablespoons pale dry sherry
1 tablespoon water	1 tablespoon water

Mix together the egg white, salt and 1 teaspoon of the cornflour (cornstarch) in a bowl. Add the fish and turn to coat.

Heat the oil in a wok or frying pan (skillet). Add the fish and fry gently until golden. Remove with a slotted spoon.

Add the spring onions (scallions) and garlic to the pan and stir-fry for 30 seconds. Return the fish slices to the pan with the sherry. Dissolve the remaining cornflour (cornstarch) in the water and add to the pan. Stir well so the sauce covers the fish evenly and cook until thickened. Serve hot.
Serves 4

Red-Cooked Fish

METRIC/IMPERIAL	AMERICAN
1 kg/2 lb whole fish (carp, bream, mullet or mackerel), cleaned and scaled	2 lb whole fish (carp, porgy, mullet or mackerel), cleaned and scaled
4 tablespoons soy sauce	$\frac{1}{4}$ cup soy sauce
15 g/$\frac{1}{2}$ oz dried wood ears	$\frac{1}{2}$ cup dried tree ears
3 tablespoons vegetable oil	3 tablespoons vegetable oil
50 g/2 oz canned bamboo shoot, drained and sliced	$\frac{1}{2}$ cup sliced canned bamboo shoot
3–4 spring onions, shredded	3–4 scallions, shredded
3 slices root ginger, shredded	3 slices ginger root, shredded
2 teaspoons cornflour, blended with 1 tablespoon water	2 teaspoons cornstarch, blended with 1 tablespoon water
Sauce:	**Sauce:**
2 tablespoons soy sauce	2 tablespoons soy sauce
2 tablespoons dry sherry	2 tablespoons pale dry sherry
2 teaspoons sugar	2 teaspoons sugar
4 tablespoons stock	$\frac{1}{4}$ cup stock

Marinate the fish in the soy sauce for 30 minutes. Soak the wood (tree) ears in warm water for 20 minutes. Drain and remove the stalks. Mix together the sauce ingredients.

Heat the oil in a wok or frying pan (skillet). When it is very hot, add the fish and fry until golden. Add the sauce, wood (tree) ears and bamboo shoot and cook for about 10 minutes. Add the spring onions (scallions) and ginger and cook until the sauce is reduced by half. Add the blended cornflour (cornstarch) and cook, stirring, until thickened.

Lift the fish onto a warmed serving dish. Pour over the sauce and serve hot.
Serves 6

Prawns (Shrimp) in Shells

METRIC/IMPERIAL	AMERICAN
225 g/8 oz Pacific or Dublin Bay prawns	½ lb jumbo shrimp
300 ml/½ pint vegetable oil	1¼ cups vegetable oil
2 tablespoons soy sauce	2 tablespoons soy sauce
2 tablespoons dry sherry	2 tablespoons pale dry sherry
1 tablespoon sugar	1 tablespoon sugar
2 spring onions, chopped	2 scallions, chopped
2 slices root ginger, chopped	2 slices ginger root, chopped
chopped parsley to garnish	chopped parsley for garnish

Trim the legs off the prawns (shrimp) but keep the body shells on.

Heat the oil in a wok or frying pan (skillet). Add the prawns (shrimp) and fry for a few seconds or until they just start to turn pink. Lift them out with a slotted spoon.

Pour off the oil, then return the prawns (shrimp) to the pan. Add the soy sauce, sherry, sugar, spring onions (scallions) and ginger. Stir-fry vigorously for a few seconds. Serve hot, garnished with parsley.
Serves 4 as a starter

Deep-Fried Spiced Fish

METRIC/IMPERIAL	AMERICAN
750 g/1½ lb whole fish (sole, cod, halibut, snapper, bream, etc), cleaned and scaled	1½ lb whole fish (sole, cod, halibut, etc), cleaned and scaled
1 teaspoon grated root ginger	1 teaspoon very finely chopped ginger root
3 spring onions, chopped	3 scallions, chopped
2 teaspoons salt	2 teaspoons salt
2 tablespoons dry sherry	2 tablespoons pale dry sherry
oil for deep-frying	oil for deep-frying
1 teaspoon ground Szechuan or black peppercorns	1 teaspoon ground Szechuan or black peppercorns
2 tablespoons sesame seed oil	2 tablespoons sesame seed oil
Garnish:	**Garnish:**
lemon slices	lemon slices
parsley sprigs	parsley sprigs
chopped spring onion	chopped scallions
glacé cherry quarters (optional)	glacé cherry quarters (optional)

Score the fish by making diagonal slashes on each side. Place the ginger, spring onions (scallions), 1 teaspoon of the salt and the sherry in a dish and add the fish. Leave to marinate for 30 minutes.

Heat the oil in a wok or deep-fryer to 180°C/350°F. Deep-fry the fish until golden brown. Drain on kitchen paper towels and place on a warmed serving dish. Sprinkle with the ground peppercorns and remaining salt. Heat the sesame seed oil and pour over the fish. Garnish with lemon slices, parsley, spring onions (scallions) and cherry quarters, if using.
Serves 6

Sautéed Prawns (Shrimp) in Sauce

METRIC/IMPERIAL	AMERICAN
450 g/1 lb Pacific or Dublin Bay prawns, shelled and deveined	1 lb jumbo shrimp, shelled and deveined
½ teaspoon salt	½ teaspoon salt
2 teaspoons dry sherry	2 teaspoons pale dry sherry
1 egg white	1 egg white
1 tablespoon cornflour	1 tablespoon cornstarch
5 tablespoons vegetable oil	⅓ cup vegetable oil
½ teaspoon crushed garlic	½ teaspoon minced garlic
3 spring onions, cut into 2.5 cm/1 inch pieces	3 scallions, cut into 1 inch pieces
1 tablespoon soy sauce	1 tablespoon soy sauce
1 teaspoon sugar	1 teaspoon sugar
1 tablespoon red wine vinegar	1 tablespoon red wine vinegar
dash of Tabasco sauce	dash of Tabasco sauce

Cut the prawns (shrimp) into 2.5 cm/1 inch pieces. Mix together the salt, sherry, egg white and cornflour (cornstarch). Add the prawns (shrimp) and toss to coat with the batter.

Heat the oil in a wok or frying pan (skillet). Add the garlic, prawns (shrimp) and spring onions (scallions) and stir-fry for 2 minutes. Add the remaining ingredients and stir well. Serve hot.
Serves 4

Sautéed Prawns (Shrimp) in Sauce (above)
Deep-Fried Spiced Fish (below)

Steamed Five Willow Fish

METRIC/IMPERIAL

750 g–1 kg/1½–2 lb
  whole fish (trout,
  bream, carp, mullet,
  etc)
2 teaspoons salt
1½ tablespoons
  vegetable oil
40 g/1½ oz lard
2 small chillis, seeded
  and shredded
6 spring onions, cut into
  5 cm/2 inch pieces
6 slices root ginger,
  shredded
1 red pepper, cored,
  seeded and shredded
2–3 pieces canned
  bamboo shoot,
  shredded
3 tablespoons soy sauce
3 tablespoons wine
  vinegar
1 tablespoon cornflour,
  blended with
  5 tablespoons stock

AMERICAN

1½–2 lb whole fish
  (trout, bream, carp,
  mullet, etc)
2 teaspoons salt
1½ tablespoons
  vegetable oil
3 tablespoons lard
2 small chilies, seeded
  and shredded
6 scallions, cut into
  2 inch pieces
6 slices ginger root,
  shredded
1 red pepper, seeded
  and shredded
2–3 pieces canned
  bamboo shoot,
  shredded
3 tablespoons soy sauce
3 tablespoons wine
  vinegar
1 tablespoon cornstarch,
  blended with
  5 tablespoons stock

Clean the fish thoroughly, leaving the head and tail intact. Rub the fish inside and out with the salt and oil, and leave for 30 minutes.

Arrange the fish on an oval heatproof serving dish and place in a steamer. Steam vigorously for 15 minutes. Melt the lard in a wok or frying pan (skillet), add the chillis and stir-fry for about 30 seconds. Add all the vegetables, soy sauce and vinegar and stir-fry for 15 seconds. Add the blended cornflour (cornstarch) and stir-fry until thickened.

Remove the vegetables from the pan with a slotted spoon and use to garnish the fish. Pour over the sauce and serve hot.
Serves 6

Fish with Bean Curd in Hot and Sour Sauce

METRIC/IMPERIAL

450 g/1 lb fish fillets
  (cod, halibut,
  snapper)
3 tablespoons soy sauce
4 tablespoons vegetable
  oil
2–3 spring onions,
  finely chopped
2–3 slices root ginger,
  finely chopped
1 garlic clove, crushed
2 cakes bean curd, each
  cut into 12 cubes
1 teaspoon salt
2 tablespoons dry sherry
1 teaspoon sugar
1 tablespoon chilli sauce
2 tablespoons wine
  vinegar
120 ml/4 fl oz water
chopped parsley to
  garnish

AMERICAN

1 lb fish fillets (cod or
  halibut)
3 tablespoons soy sauce
¼ cup vegetable oil
2–3 scallions, finely
  chopped
2–3 slices ginger root,
  finely chopped
1 garlic clove, minced
2 cakes bean curd, each
  cut into 12 cubes
1 teaspoon salt
2 tablespoons pale dry
  sherry
1 teaspoon sugar
1 tablespoon chili sauce
2 tablespoons wine
  vinegar
½ cup water
chopped parsley for
  garnish

Cut the fish into 5 × 2.5 cm/2 × 1 inch pieces. Sprinkle with 1 tablespoon of the soy sauce and leave to marinate for about 20 minutes.

Heat 3 tablespoons of the oil in a wok or frying pan (skillet). Add the fish pieces and fry until golden. Remove from the pan and set aside.

Heat the remaining oil in the pan. Add the spring onions (scallions), ginger and garlic and fry for a few seconds. Add the bean curd cubes, fish pieces, salt, sherry, sugar, chilli sauce, vinegar, water and remaining soy sauce. Bring to the boil, then simmer for 10 minutes.

Serve hot, garnished with chopped parsley.
Serves 4

Carp with Sweet and Sour Sauce

METRIC/IMPERIAL	AMERICAN
15 g/½ oz dried wood ears	½ cup dried tree ears
1 carp, weighing 750 g–1 kg/1½–2 lb	1 carp, weighing 1½–2 lb
2 teaspoons salt	2 teaspoons salt
3 tablespoons plain flour	3 tablespoons all-purpose flour
4 tablespoons oil	¼ cup oil
2–3 spring onions, shredded	2–3 scallions, shredded
2 slices root ginger, shredded	2 slices ginger root, shredded
1 garlic clove, finely chopped	1 garlic clove, finely chopped
15 g/½ oz canned bamboo shoot, drained and thinly sliced	2 tablespoons thinly sliced canned bamboo shoot
50 g/2 oz canned water chestnuts, drained and thinly sliced	¼ cup canned water chestnuts, thinly sliced
1 red pepper, cored, seeded and shredded	1 red pepper, seeded and shredded
3 tablespoons wine vinegar	3 tablespoons wine vinegar
Sauce:	**Sauce:**
3 tablespoons sugar	3 tablespoons sugar
2 tablespoons soy sauce	2 tablespoons soy sauce
2 tablespoons dry sherry	2 tablespoons pale dry sherry
2 teaspoons cornflour	2 teaspoons cornstarch
150 ml/¼ pint chicken stock or water	⅔ cup chicken stock or water
1 teaspoon chilli sauce	1 teaspoon chili sauce

Soak the wood (tree) ears in warm water for 20 minutes. Drain and slice very thinly, discarding the hard bits.

Clean the fish thoroughly, removing the fins and tail but leaving the head on. Slash both sides of the fish diagonally at 5 mm/¼ inch intervals through to the bone. Dry thoroughly, then rub the fish inside and out with half the salt. Coat completely with the flour.

Heat the oil in a wok or frying pan (skillet) until very hot. Lower the heat a little, add the fish and fry for about 3 to 4 minutes on each side until golden and crisp, turning carefully. Drain and transfer carefully to a warmed serving dish. Keep hot.

Mix the sauce ingredients together. Add the spring onions (scallions), ginger and garlic to the oil remaining in the pan. Stir in the wood (tree) ears, bamboo shoot, water chestnuts, red pepper, vinegar and remaining salt. Add the sauce mixture and cook, stirring, until thickened. Pour over the fish and serve.
Serves 6

Braised Fish with Spring Onions (Scallions) and Ginger

METRIC/IMPERIAL	AMERICAN
1 fish (mullet, bream, etc.), weighing 750 g–1 kg/1½–2 lb	1 fish (mullet, sea bass, etc.), weighing 1½–2 lb
1 teaspoon salt	1 teaspoon salt
2 tablespoons plain flour	2 tablespoons all-purpose flour
3 tablespoons vegetable oil	3 tablespoons vegetable oil
3–4 spring onions, cut into 2.5 cm/1 inch lengths	3–4 scallions, cut into 1 inch lengths
2–3 slices root ginger, shredded	2–3 slices ginger root, shredded
Sauce:	**Sauce:**
2 tablespoons soy sauce	2 tablespoons soy sauce
2 tablespoons dry sherry	2 tablespoons pale dry sherry
150 ml/¼ pint chicken stock	⅔ cup chicken stock
1 teaspoon cornflour	1 teaspoon cornstarch
freshly ground black pepper	freshly ground black pepper

Clean the fish thoroughly, leaving the fins, tail and head on. Slash both sides of the fish diagonally at 5 mm/¼ inch intervals through to the bone. Rub the fish inside and out with the salt, then coat completely with the flour.

Heat the oil in a wok or frying pan (skillet) until very hot. Lower the heat a little, add the fish and fry for about 2 minutes on each side or until golden and crisp, turning carefully. Remove from the pan and set aside.

Mix the sauce ingredients together. Increase the heat and add the spring onions (scallions) and ginger to the oil remaining in pan. Stir-fry for a few seconds, then stir in the sauce and return the fish to the pan. Simmer for a few minutes, then carefully transfer the fish to a warmed serving dish and pour over the sauce. Serve hot.
Serves 6

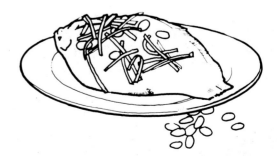

Poultry Dishes

Chicken Wings Stuffed with Ham

METRIC/IMPERIAL	AMERICAN
5 Chinese dried mushrooms	5 Chinese dried mushrooms
12 chicken wings	12 chicken wings
3 tablespoons soy sauce	3 tablespoons soy sauce
oil for deep-frying	oil for deep-frying
350 ml/12 fl oz chicken stock or water	1½ cups chicken stock or water
1 tablespoon dry sherry	1 tablespoon pale dry sherry
1–2 slices cooked ham, shredded	1–2 slices cooked ham, shredded
3 spring onions, chopped	3 scallions, chopped
1 tablespoon sugar	1 tablespoon sugar
1 tablespoon cornflour, blended with 1 tablespoon water	1 tablespoon cornstarch, blended with 1 tablespoon water

Soak the mushrooms in warm water for 20 minutes. Squeeze dry and remove the hard stalks, then cut the mushroom caps in half.

Cut off the pointed ends of the chicken wings. Sprinkle with 1 tablespoon of the soy sauce and leave for 30 minutes. Heat the oil in a wok or deep-fryer to 180°C/350°F. Deep-fry the chicken wings until golden brown. Drain on kitchen paper towels.

Bring the stock or water to the boil in a large pan. Add the chicken wings, remaining soy sauce and the sherry; simmer for 30 minutes.

Remove the chicken wings from the pan and allow to cool, then carefully remove the bones, leaving the chicken wings whole. Insert a little ham into the cavity of each chicken wing. Return the stock mixture to the boil and add the spring onions (scallions), mushrooms, chicken wings and sugar. Simmer for 5 minutes. Add the blended cornflour (cornstarch) and simmer, stirring, until thickened. Serve hot.
Serves 4

Deep-Fried Chicken with Peppery Hot Sauce (above)
Chicken Wings Stuffed with Ham (below)

Deep-Fried Chicken with Peppery Hot Sauce

METRIC/IMPERIAL	AMERICAN
750 g/1½ lb boned chicken	1½ lb boneless chicken
3 tablespoons soy sauce	3 tablespoons soy sauce
1 tablespoon dry sherry	1 tablespoon pale dry sherry
1 teaspoon Szechuan or black peppercorns	1 teaspoon Szechuan or black peppercorns
4 tablespoons chopped spring onions	¼ cup chopped scallions
1 egg, beaten	1 egg, beaten
5 tablespoons cornflour	5 tablespoons cornstarch
2 tablespoons plain flour	2 tablespoons all-purpose flour
oil for deep-frying	oil for deep-frying
Peppery hot sauce:	**Peppery hot sauce:**
2 tablespoons chopped spring onions	2 tablespoons chopped scallions
1 tablespoon sesame seed oil	1 tablespoon sesame seed oil
1 tablespoon sesame seeds	1 tablespoon sesame seeds
2 tablespoons red wine vinegar	2 tablespoons red wine vinegar
3 tablespoons soy sauce	3 tablespoons soy sauce
3 tablespoons chicken stock	3 tablespoons chicken stock
1 teaspoon ground Szechuan or black peppercorns	1 teaspoon ground Szechuan or black peppercorns
2 teaspoons hot oil	2 teaspoons hot oil

Cut the chicken into 2.5 cm/1 inch pieces. Mix together the soy sauce, sherry, peppercorns and spring onions (scallions) in a bowl. Add the chicken and leave to marinate for 15 minutes.

Meanwhile, mix all the sauce ingredients together in a small serving bowl.

Beat together the egg, cornflour (cornstarch) and flour to make a smooth batter. Dip the chicken pieces into the batter to coat well.

Heat the oil in a wok or deep-fryer to 180°C/350°F. Deep-fry the chicken pieces a few at a time until crisp and golden. Drain well on kitchen paper towels.

Arrange on a warmed serving dish. Serve hot, with the peppery hot sauce handed separately.
Serves 6

Lotus-White Chicken

METRIC/IMPERIAL	AMERICAN
5 egg whites	5 egg whites
120 ml/4 fl oz chicken stock	½ cup chicken stock
1 teaspoon salt	1 teaspoon salt
1 teaspoon dry sherry	1 teaspoon pale dry sherry
2 teaspoons cornflour	2 teaspoons cornstarch
100 g/4 oz chicken breast meat, skinned and finely chopped	½ cup skinned and finely chopped chicken breast meat
oil for deep-frying	oil for deep-frying
Garnish:	**Garnish:**
1–2 tablespoons cooked green peas	1–2 tablespoons cooked green peas
25 g/1 oz cooked ham, shredded	1 slice cooked ham, shredded

Put the egg whites in a bowl. Stir in 3 tablespoons of the stock, the salt, sherry and half the cornflour (cornstarch). Add the chicken and mix well.

Heat the oil in a wok or deep-fryer to 180°C/350°F, then gently pour in about one third of the chicken mixture. Deep-fry for 10 seconds until the mixture begins to rise to the surface, then carefully turn over. Deep-fry until golden, then remove from the pan with a slotted spoon, drain and place on a warmed serving dish. Keep hot while cooking the remaining chicken mixture in the same way.

Heat the remaining stock in a small pan. Mix the remaining cornflour (cornstarch) to a paste with a little cold water, add to the stock and simmer, stirring, until thickened. Pour over the chicken.

Garnish with the peas and shredded ham and serve immediately.
Serves 2

Fried Chicken Legs

METRIC/IMPERIAL	AMERICAN
6 chicken legs	6 chicken legs
2 tablespoons soy sauce	2 tablespoons soy sauce
1 tablespoon dry sherry	1 tablespoon pale dry sherry
½ teaspoon freshly ground black pepper	½ teaspoon freshly ground black pepper
2 tablespoons cornflour	2 tablespoons cornstarch
600 ml/1 pint oil for deep-frying	2½ cups oil for deep-frying
1 tablespoon finely chopped spring onion	1 tablespoon finely chopped scallion

Chop each chicken leg into 2 or 3 pieces, then mix with the soy sauce, sherry and pepper in a bowl. Leave to marinate for about 20 minutes, turning occasionally.

Coat each piece of chicken with cornflour (cornstarch). Heat the oil in a wok or deep-fryer to 180°C/350°F. Lower the heat, add the chicken pieces and deep-fry until golden. Remove from the pan with a slotted spoon and drain on kitchen paper towels.

Pour off all but 1 tablespoon oil, then add the spring onion (scallion) to the pan with the chicken pieces. Stir-fry for about 2 minutes. Serve hot.
Serves 6

Chicken in Foil

METRIC/IMPERIAL	AMERICAN
450 g/1 lb chicken breast meat, skinned	1 lb chicken breast meat, skinned
3 spring onions, white part only	3 scallions, white part only
¼ teaspoon salt	¼ teaspoon salt
1 tablespoon soy sauce	1 tablespoon soy sauce
1 teaspoon sugar	1 teaspoon sugar
1 teaspoon dry sherry	1 teaspoon pale dry sherry
1 teaspoon sesame seed oil	1 teaspoon sesame seed oil
4 tablespoons vegetable oil	¼ cup vegetable oil
Garnish:	**Garnish:**
shredded spring onion	shredded scallion
finely chopped red pepper	finely chopped red pepper

Cut the chicken into 12 roughly equal-sized pieces. Cut each spring onion (scallion) into 4 pieces. Combine the chicken and spring onions (scallions) with the salt, soy sauce, sugar, sherry and sesame seed oil in a bowl. Leave to marinate for about 20 minutes.

Cut 12 squares of foil large enough to wrap around the chicken pieces 4 times. Brush the pieces of foil with oil, then place a piece of chicken on each. Top with a slice of spring onion (scallion), then wrap the foil around the chicken to make a parcel, making sure that no meat is exposed.

Heat the oil in a wok or frying pan (skillet). Add the chicken parcels and fry for about 2 minutes on each side. Remove and leave to drain on a wok rack or in a strainer for a few minutes; turn off the heat.

Reheat the oil. When it is very hot, return the chicken parcels to the pan and fry for 1 minute only. Serve hot in the foil, garnished with shredded spring onion (scallion) and red pepper.
Serves 4

Stir-Fried Chicken with Bean Sprouts

METRIC/IMPERIAL	AMERICAN
350 g/12 oz skinned and boned chicken breast	¾ lb boneless chicken breast, skinned
1 teaspoon dry sherry	1 teaspoon pale dry sherry
1 teaspoon salt	1 teaspoon salt
2 teaspoons cornflour	2 teaspoons cornstarch
1 egg white	1 egg white
6 tablespoons vegetable oil	6 tablespoons vegetable oil
225 g/8 oz bean sprouts	½ lb bean sprouts
½ teaspoon sugar	½ teaspoon sugar
2–3 spring onions, finely shredded, to garnish	2–3 scallions, finely shredded, for garnish

Cut the chicken into strips. Mix together the sherry, ½ teaspoon of the salt, the cornflour (cornstarch) and egg white in a bowl. Add the chicken and toss to coat thoroughly.

Heat 4 tablespoons of the oil in a wok or frying pan (skillet). Add the chicken and cook for about 3 minutes. Transfer to a plate and keep on one side.

Add the remaining oil to the pan and reheat. Add the bean sprouts and stir-fry for 30 seconds. Return the chicken to the pan with the sugar and remaining salt and stir-fry for a few seconds.

Transfer to a warmed serving dish and garnish with the shredded spring onions (scallions).
Serves 4

Stewed Chicken with Chestnuts

METRIC/IMPERIAL	AMERICAN
1 chicken, weighing 1 kg/2 lb, boned	1 chicken, weighing 2 lb, boned
6 tablespoons soy sauce	6 tablespoons soy sauce
1 tablespoon dry sherry	1 tablespoon pale dry sherry
2 tablespoons vegetable oil	2 tablespoons vegetable oil
2 slices root ginger, chopped	2 slices ginger root, chopped
4 spring onions, chopped	4 scallions, chopped
450 g/1 lb chestnuts, peeled and skinned	1 lb chestnuts, peeled and skinned
450 ml/¾ pint water	2 cups water
1 tablespoon sugar	1 tablespoon sugar

Cut the chicken into 3.5 cm/1½ inch pieces. Mix together the soy sauce and sherry, add the chicken and leave to marinate for 15 minutes.

Heat the oil in a large pan. Add the chicken mixture, ginger and half the spring onions (scallions) and stir-fry until the chicken is golden. Add the chestnuts, water and sugar. Bring to the boil, cover and simmer for 40 minutes, or until tender.

Serve hot, garnished with the remaining spring onions (scallions).
Serves 4
Note: if fresh chestnuts are unobtainable, canned or dried ones may be used. Canned chestnuts should be drained and added to the chicken mixture 10 minutes before the end of the cooking time; dried chestnuts should be soaked in warm water overnight then used as fresh chestnuts.

Oil-Basted Chicken

METRIC/IMPERIAL	AMERICAN
1 chicken, weighing 1.5 kg/3–3½ lb	1 chicken, weighing 3–3½ lb
2 tablespoons soy sauce	2 tablespoons soy sauce
1 tablespoon dry sherry	1 tablespoon pale dry sherry
1.2 litres/2 pints oil for deep-frying	5 cups oil for deep-frying
Sauce:	**Sauce:**
2 spring onions, finely chopped	2 scallions, finely chopped
2 slices root ginger, finely chopped	2 slices ginger root, finely chopped
1 garlic clove, finely chopped	1 garlic clove, finely chopped
2 tablespoons vinegar	2 tablespoons vinegar
1½ tablespoons sugar	1½ tablespoons sugar
1 tablespoon yellow bean sauce	1 tablespoon yellow bean sauce

Wash and clean the chicken thoroughly, then plunge into a large pan of boiling water. Boil rapidly for 2 to 3 minutes, remove and drain.

Mix together the soy sauce and sherry and brush over the chicken. Leave to marinate for about 20 minutes. Meanwhile, mix together the sauce ingredients in a small pan.

Heat the oil in a wok or deep-fryer. Add the chicken and cook for 20 to 30 minutes until browned on all sides, basting constantly.

Remove the chicken from the pan, chop into small pieces, and arrange on a warmed serving dish. Add any remaining marinade to the sauce mixture, heat through, then pour over the chicken. Serve hot.
Serves 6

Diced Chicken with Celery

METRIC/IMPERIAL
3–4 Chinese dried
  mushrooms
225 g/8 oz chicken
  breast meat, skinned
  and diced
½ teaspoon salt
1 egg white
1 tablespoon cornflour
5 tablespoons vegetable
  oil
2 slices root ginger,
  finely chopped
2–3 spring onions,
  finely chopped
1 small head celery,
  diced
100 g/4 oz canned
  bamboo shoot,
  drained and diced
1 red pepper, cored,
  seeded and diced
3 tablespoons soy sauce
1 teaspoon dry sherry
chopped coriander
  leaves or parsley to
  garnish

AMERICAN
3–4 Chinese dried
  mushrooms
1 cup skinned and diced
  chicken breast meat
½ teaspoon salt
1 egg white
1 tablespoon cornstarch
⅓ cup vegetable oil
2 slices ginger root,
  finely chopped
2–3 scallions, finely
  chopped
1 small bunch celery,
  diced
1 cup diced canned
  bamboo shoot
1 red pepper, seeded
  and diced
3 tablespoons soy sauce
1 teaspoon pale dry
  sherry
chopped coriander
  leaves or parsley for
  garnish

Soak the mushrooms in warm water for 20 minutes. Squeeze dry, remove the hard stalks then dice the mushroom caps.

Sprinkle the chicken with the salt, dip into the egg white, then coat with the cornflour (cornstarch).

Heat the oil in a wok or frying pan (skillet). Add the chicken and stir-fry for 2 minutes. Remove with a slotted spoon and set aside.

Increase the heat to high and add the ginger and spring onions (scallions) to the pan. Add the mushrooms and remaining vegetables and stir-fry for 1 minute.

Return the chicken to the pan, add the soy sauce and sherry and cook for 1 minute until the liquid thickens, stirring constantly. Serve hot, garnished with coriander or parsley.
Serves 2

Lemon Chicken

METRIC/IMPERIAL
5–6 Chinese dried
  mushrooms
1 chicken, weighing
  1.5–2 kg/3–4 lb,
  boned
1½ teaspoons salt
freshly ground black
  pepper
5 tablespoons vegetable
  oil
15 g/½ oz lard
4 slices root ginger,
  chopped
1 red pepper, cored,
  seeded and shredded
shredded rind of 2
  lemons
5 spring onions, thinly
  sliced
4 tablespoons dry sherry
1½ teaspoons sugar
2 tablespoons soy sauce
  (preferably light)
1 teaspoon cornflour,
  blended with
  1 tablespoon water
1–2 tablespoons lemon
  juice

AMERICAN
5–6 Chinese dried
  mushrooms
1 chicken, weighing
  3–4 lb, boned
1½ teaspoons salt
freshly ground black
  pepper
⅓ cup vegetable oil
1 tablespoon lard
4 slices ginger root,
  chopped
1 red pepper, seeded
  and shredded
shredded rind of 2
  lemons
5 scallions, thinly sliced
¼ cup pale dry sherry
1½ teaspoons sugar
2 tablespoons soy sauce
  (preferably light)
1 teaspoon cornstarch,
  blended with
  1 tablespoon water
1–2 tablespoons lemon
  juice

Soak the mushrooms in warm water for 20 minutes. Squeeze dry and remove the hard stalks, then shred the mushroom caps.

Cut the chicken into bite-sized pieces and mix with the salt and pepper to taste and 1½ tablespoons of the oil. Heat the remaining oil in a wok or frying pan (skillet). Add the chicken and stir-fry for 2 minutes; remove and keep warm.

Add the lard to the pan. When the fat has melted, add the ginger, red pepper and mushrooms. Stir-fry for 1 minute. Add the lemon rind and spring onions (scallions). Stir-fry for 30 seconds.

Sprinkle in the sherry, sugar and soy sauce and bring to the boil, then stir in the blended cornflour (cornstarch). Return the chicken to the pan and cook, stirring, for 1 minute. Sprinkle in the lemon juice and serve hot.
Serves 6 to 8

Lemon Chicken

Soy Chicken

METRIC/IMPERIAL	AMERICAN
1 chicken, weighing 1.5 kg/3–3½ lb	1 chicken, weighing 3–3½ lb
1 teaspoon freshly ground black pepper	1 teaspoon freshly ground black pepper
2 teaspoons finely chopped root ginger	2 teaspoons finely chopped ginger root
5 tablespoons soy sauce	⅓ cup soy sauce
3 tablespoons dry sherry	3 tablespoons pale dry sherry
1 tablespoon brown sugar	1 tablespoon brown sugar
3 tablespoons vegetable oil	3 tablespoons vegetable oil
300 ml/½ pint chicken stock or water	1¼ cups chicken stock or water
coriander leaves or parsley to garnish	coriander leaves or parsley to garnish

Wash the chicken, dry thoroughly and rub inside and out with the pepper and ginger. Mix together the soy sauce, sherry and sugar. Spoon over the chicken and leave to marinate for at least 3 hours, turning occasionally.

Heat the oil in a large pan, add the whole chicken and fry, turning, until lightly browned on all sides.

Dilute the marinade with the stock or water and add to the pan. Bring to the boil, cover and simmer for 45 minutes, turning the chicken several times during cooking; take care not to break the skin.

Chop the chicken into small pieces. Arrange on a warmed serving dish and pour over 2 tablespoons of the sauce. Garnish with coriander or parsley. Serve hot as a main course, or cold as a starter.
Serves 6 to 8
Note: do not discard the cooking sauce; it can be stored in the refrigerator for future use.

Smoked Chicken

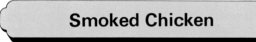

METRIC/IMPERIAL	AMERICAN
2 tablespoons Szechuan or black peppercorns	2 tablespoons Szechuan or black peppercorns
2 tablespoons salt	2 tablespoons salt
1 chicken, weighing 1 kg/2 lb	1 chicken, weighing 2 lb
100 g/4 oz sugar	½ cup sugar
40 g/1½ oz tea leaves	½ cup tea leaves
1 tablespoon sesame seed oil	1 tablespoon sesame seed oil

Toast the peppercorns in a pan, then crush them coarsely and mix with the salt. Rub the chicken inside and out with the peppercorn mixture. Leave to stand for a few hours.

Place a large sheet of foil in a roasting pan so the foil hangs well over the sides; sprinkle with the sugar and tea leaves. Put a rack in the pan and place the chicken on it. Bring the foil up over the chicken and fold together to seal. Cook in a preheated moderately hot oven (190°C/375°F, Gas Mark 5) for 30 minutes.

Unwrap the chicken and brush with the sesame seed oil. Return to the oven and roast, uncovered, for a further 5 to 10 minutes or until golden brown. Cut the chicken into serving pieces and serve hot.
Serves 4

Shredded Chicken with Peppers

METRIC/IMPERIAL	AMERICAN
225 g/8 oz chicken breast meat, skinned and shredded	1 cup shredded, skinned chicken breast meat
½ teaspoon salt	½ teaspoon salt
1 tablespoon soy sauce	1 tablespoon soy sauce
1 egg white	1 egg white
1 tablespoon cornflour	1 tablespoon cornstarch
5 tablespoons vegetable oil	⅓ cup vegetable oil
2 slices root ginger, shredded	2 slices ginger root, shredded
2–3 spring onions, shredded	2–3 scallions, shredded
1 chilli, seeded and shredded	1 chili, seeded and shredded
1 green pepper, cored, seeded and shredded	1 green pepper, seeded and shredded
1 red pepper, cored, seeded and shredded	1 red pepper, seeded and shredded
2–3 celery sticks, shredded	2–3 celery stalks, shredded
2 tablespoons black bean sauce	2 tablespoons salted black beans

Put the chicken in a bowl with the salt, soy sauce, egg white and cornflour (cornstarch) and mix well.

Heat the oil in a wok or frying pan (skillet), add the chicken and stir-fry for 2 minutes. Remove from the pan with a slotted spoon and set aside.

Increase the heat to high. When the oil starts to smoke, add the ginger, spring onions (scallions), chilli, peppers and celery. Stir well, add bean sauce (salted black beans) and cook for a few seconds.

Return the chicken to the pan, mix well, then stir-fry for about 1 to 1½ minutes until the meat is tender, but the vegetables are still crisp. Serve hot.
Serves 2

Chicken Wings with Broccoli

METRIC/IMPERIAL	AMERICAN
12 chicken wings	12 chicken wings
4 spring onions, finely chopped	4 scallions, finely chopped
2 slices root ginger, finely chopped	2 slices ginger root, finely chopped
1 tablespoon lemon juice	1 tablespoon lemon juice
1 tablespoon soy sauce	1 tablespoon soy sauce
1½ teaspoons salt	1½ teaspoons salt
1 tablespoon dry sherry	1 tablespoon pale dry sherry
4 tablespoons vegetable oil	¼ cup vegetable oil
225 g/8 oz broccoli, divided into florets	½ lb broccoli, divided into florets
50 g/2 oz tomatoes, skinned and chopped	¼ cup skinned and chopped tomatoes
1 tablespoon cornflour, blended with	1 tablespoon cornstarch, blended with
2 tablespoons water	2 tablespoons water

Trim and discard the tips of the chicken wings, then cut each wing into 2 pieces by breaking the joint.

Put the chicken in a bowl with the spring onions (scallions), ginger, lemon juice, soy sauce, ½ teaspoon of the salt and the sherry. Stir well and leave to marinate for about 20 minutes.

Heat 2 tablespoons of the oil in a wok or frying pan (skillet). Add the broccoli and remaining salt and stir-fry until tender but still crisp. Arrange the broccoli around the edge of a warmed serving dish and keep hot.

Remove the chicken pieces, reserving the marinade. Heat the remaining oil in the pan, add the chicken and fry until golden. Remove from the pan with a slotted spoon and drain on kitchen paper towels.

Add the tomatoes to the pan and stir-fry until reduced to a pulp. Return the chicken to the pan with the marinade. Cook for about 2 minutes, then add the blended cornflour (cornstarch) and cook, stirring constantly, until thickened. Spoon into the centre of the serving dish. Serve immediately.
Serves 4

Braised Chicken Wings

METRIC/IMPERIAL	AMERICAN
4 Chinese dried mushrooms	4 Chinese dried mushrooms
12 chicken wings	12 chicken wings
2 tablespoons vegetable oil	2 tablespoons vegetable oil
2 spring onions, finely chopped	2 scallions, finely chopped
2 slices root ginger, finely chopped	2 slices ginger root, finely chopped
2 tablespoons soy sauce	2 tablespoons soy sauce
2 tablespoons dry sherry	2 tablespoons pale dry sherry
1 tablespoon sugar	1 tablespoon sugar
½ teaspoon five-spice powder	½ teaspoon five-spice powder
350 ml/12 fl oz water	1½ cups water
175 g/6 oz canned bamboo shoot, drained and cut into chunks	1½ cups canned bamboo shoot, cut into chunks
2 teaspoons cornflour, blended with	2 teaspoons cornstarch, blended with
1 tablespoon water	1 tablespoon water

Soak the mushrooms in warm water for 20 minutes. Squeeze dry, remove the hard stalks and cut the mushroom caps into small pieces.

Trim and discard the tips of the chicken wings, then cut each wing in half by breaking the joint.

Heat the oil in a wok or frying pan (skillet) until it reaches smoking point. Add the spring onions (scallions) and ginger, then the chicken wings. Stir-fry until the chicken is lightly browned all over, then add the soy sauce, sherry, sugar, five-spice powder and water.

Lower the heat and cook gently until the liquid has reduced by about half. Add the mushrooms and bamboo shoot and continue cooking until the juice has almost completely evaporated. Remove the bamboo shoot chunks, rinse, drain and arrange around the edge of a warmed serving dish.

Add the blended cornflour (cornstarch) to the pan and cook, stirring constantly, until thickened. Place the chicken mixture in the centre of the bamboo shoot. Serve hot.
Serves 4

Peking Roast Duck

METRIC/IMPERIAL
1 duck, weighing
  2 kg/4½ lb
3 tablespoons honey or
  black treacle
2 tablespoons red wine
  vinegar
2 tablespoons dry sherry
250 ml/8 fl oz hot water
Mandarin pancakes:
225 g/8 oz plain flour
250 ml/8 fl oz boiling
  water
2 tablespoons sesame
  seed oil
To serve:
120 ml/4 fl oz soy bean
  paste or hoisin sauce
1 cucumber, sliced
4 spring onions,
  shredded

AMERICAN
1 duck, weighing 4½ lb
3 tablespoons honey or
  molasses
2 tablespoons red wine
  vinegar
2 tablespoons pale dry
  sherry
1 cup hot water
Mandarin pancakes:
2 cups all-purpose flour
1 cup boiling water
2 tablespoons sesame
  seed oil
To serve:
½ cup bean sauce or
  hoisin sauce
1 cucumber, sliced
4 scallions, shredded

Place the duck in a large saucepan and cover with boiling water. Boil for 5 minutes, then drain and cool under running water. Dry on kitchen paper towels.

Combine the honey or treacle (molasses), vinegar, sherry and hot water. Brush the duck skin with this mixture. Brace the wings away from the body with two skewers. Hang the duck by the neck in a well-ventilated place to dry overnight.

Place the duck on a rack in a roasting pan and cook in a preheated moderately hot oven (200°C/400°F, Gas Mark 6) for 30 minutes. Lower the heat to 190°C/375°F, Gas Mark 5 and cook for a further 40 minutes or until the duck is tender.

Meanwhile, make the Mandarin pancakes: sift the flour into a bowl. Add the boiling water a little at a time, beating well with a wooden spoon. Knead the dough for 5 to 6 minutes, then cover and leave to rest for 10 minutes.

Form the dough into a long roll about 5 cm/ 2 inches in diameter. Cut the roll into 1 cm/½ inch slices. Roll the slices into thin 15 cm/6 in diameter pancakes. Brush one side of each pancake with sesame seed oil and sandwich together in pairs, oiled sides facing inwards.

Heat a heavy, ungreased frying pan (skillet). Place a double-pancake in the pan and cook for 3 minutes on each side. (Brown spots will appear and some parts will start to bubble when the pancake is cooked.) Remove from the pan and cool slightly. Pull the two pancakes apart and fold each one in half, oiled side inwards. Stack on a heatproof dish and keep hot while cooking the remaining pancakes.

When all the pancakes are cooked, place in a steamer and steam for 10 minutes. Arrange on a warmed serving dish, cover with foil and keep warm.

To serve: cut off the crispy skin from the breast, sides and back of the duck and cut into 5 × 7.5 cm/ 2 × 3 inch slices. Arrange on a warmed serving dish.

Cut the wings and drumsticks from the duck. Slice the meat from the breast and carcass and arrange on a warmed serving dish, with the drumsticks and wings.

To eat: spread a little soy bean paste (sauce) or hoisin sauce onto a pancake. Place two pieces of cucumber and a little shredded spring onion (scallion) in the centre. Top with a slice of meat and a slice of duck skin then roll up.
Serves 6
Note: Mandarin pancakes will keep in the refrigerator for 2 to 3 days, but should be steamed again for 7 to 8 minutes if they are to be kept for any length of time before serving.

Ready-made pancakes are available if you prefer.

Peking Roast Duck

Diced Chicken with Brown Bean Sauce

METRIC/IMPERIAL
3 Chinese dried
  mushrooms
350 g/12 oz chicken
  meat, skinned
pinch of salt
2 teaspoons dry sherry
2 teaspoons cornflour
7 tablespoons oil
1 garlic clove, crushed
50 g/2 oz canned
  bamboo shoot,
  drained and diced
1 green pepper, cored,
  seeded and diced
2 tablespoons soy bean
  paste or hoisin sauce,
  blended with
  2 tablespoons water

AMERICAN
3 Chinese dried
  mushrooms
¾ lb boneless chicken,
  skinned
pinch of salt
2 teaspoons pale dry
  sherry
2 teaspoons cornstarch
7 tablespoons oil
1 garlic clove, minced
¼ cup diced canned
  bamboo shoot
½ cup diced green
  pepper
2 tablespoons bean
  sauce or hoisin sauce,
  blended with
  2 tablespoons water

Soak the mushrooms in warm water for 20 minutes. Squeeze dry and discard the stalks. Cut the mushroom caps into 2.5 cm/1 inch cubes.

Cut the chicken into 2.5 cm/1 inch cubes. Sprinkle with the salt, sherry and cornflour (cornstarch) and leave to marinate for 15 minutes.

Heat 5 tablespoons of the oil in a wok or frying pan (skillet). Add the chicken and stir-fry until golden brown. Transfer to a plate.

Add the remaining oil to the pan and heat. Add the garlic and stir-fry for 1 minute. Add the mushrooms, bamboo shoot and green pepper and stir-fry for a few seconds. Add the chicken with the blended bean paste (sauce) or hoisin sauce and stir well. Serve hot.
Serves 2 to 4

Onion Duck

METRIC/IMPERIAL
4 Chinese dried
  mushrooms
1 duckling, weighing
  2–2.25 kg/4½–5¼ lb
120 ml/4 fl oz soy sauce
3 tablespoons sugar
100 g/4 oz canned
  bamboo shoot,
  drained and sliced
25 g/1 oz lard
3 spring onions, finely
  chopped

AMERICAN
4 Chinese dried
  mushrooms
1 duckling, weighing
  4½–5¼ lb
½ cup soy sauce
3 tablespoons sugar
1 cup sliced canned
  bamboo shoot
2 tablespoons lard
3 scallions, finely
  chopped

Soak the mushrooms in warm water for 20 minutes. Squeeze dry and remove the hard stalks.

Put the duckling in a large pan, cover with cold water and bring to the boil. Remove from the pan and rinse under cold water. Skim the surface of the cooking water, then return the duckling to the pan.

Add more fresh water to cover the duckling if necessary and bring back to the boil. Add the soy sauce, sugar and mushrooms. Cover and cook gently for 2½ hours, turning the duckling halfway through cooking. Add the bamboo shoot and simmer for a further 30 minutes.

Transfer the duckling to a warmed serving dish. Drain the mushrooms and bamboo shoot and arrange around the duckling.

Heat the lard in a separate pan, add the spring onions (scallions) and fry for 1 to 2 minutes. Pour over the duckling and serve hot.
Serves 6 to 8

Oil-Braised Duck

METRIC/IMPERIAL
1 duckling, weighing
  1.75–2 kg/4–4¾ lb
4 tablespoons orange
  juice
2 tablespoons sugar
4 tablespoons soy sauce
4 teaspoons salt
4 tablespoons dry sherry
1 tablespoon vinegar
½ teaspoon five-spice
  powder
1 slice root ginger
600 ml/1 pint chicken
  stock
1.2 litres/2 pints oil for
  deep-frying

AMERICAN
1 duckling, weighing
  4–4¾ lb
¼ cup orange juice
2 tablespoons sugar
¼ cup soy sauce
4 teaspoons salt
¼ cup pale dry sherry
1 tablespoon vinegar
½ teaspoon five-spice
  powder
1 slice ginger root
2½ cups chicken stock
5 cups oil for deep-
  frying

Plunge the duckling into a pan of boiling water. Leave for a few minutes, then drain and place in a clean pan with the remaining ingredients. Bring to the boil, cover with a tight-fitting lid and simmer for 45 minutes, turning the duckling at least twice during cooking. Remove from the pan, drain and dry thoroughly. Leave the cooking liquid simmering to reduce and thicken.

Heat the oil in a wok or deep-fryer. Add the duckling and cook until browned on all sides. Return to the simmering liquid and turn it several times to coat with the sauce.

Remove duckling from the pan and cut into small pieces. Rearrange on a warmed serving dish and pour the remaining sauce over the top. Serve hot.
Serves 6

Pan-Fried Chicken Breast

METRIC/IMPERIAL

1 large chicken breast,
  skinned and boned
1–2 spring onions,
  chopped
1 slice root ginger, finely
  chopped
1 tablespoon dry sherry
2 teaspoons salt
1 egg, beaten
2 teaspoons cornflour
3 tablespoons vegetable
  oil
1 small lettuce
Sauce:
1 tablespoon tomato
  purée
1 teaspoon sugar
1 teaspoon sesame seed
  oil
1 tablespoon water

AMERICAN

1 large chicken breast,
  skinned and boned
1–2 scallions, chopped
1 slice ginger root, finely
  chopped
1 tablespoon pale dry
  sherry
2 teaspoons salt
1 egg, beaten
2 teaspoons cornstarch
3 tablespoons vegetable
  oil
1 small head of lettuce
Sauce:
1 tablespoon tomato
  paste
1 teaspoon sugar
1 teaspoon sesame seed
  oil
1 tablespoon water

Cut the chicken into thin rectangular slices and place in a bowl. Add the spring onion (scallion), ginger, sherry and salt and mix well. Leave to marinate for about 20 minutes.

Stir the egg into the marinated chicken, then sprinkle with the cornflour (cornstarch) and toss to coat thoroughly. Heat the oil in a wok or frying pan (skillet). Add the chicken mixture and fry until tender and golden on all sides. Remove from the pan with a slotted spoon and arrange on a bed of lettuce.

Mix together the sauce ingredients. Add to the pan in which the chicken was cooked and heat through, then either pour over the chicken, or serve as a dip. Serve hot.
Serves 2 to 4

Steamed Chicken with Chinese Mushrooms

METRIC/IMPERIAL

450 g/1 lb boned
  chicken (breasts and
  thighs), cut into small
  pieces
1½ tablespoons soy
  sauce
1 tablespoon dry sherry
1 teaspoon sugar
1 teaspoon cornflour
4 Chinese dried
  mushrooms
1 tablespoon vegetable
  oil
2 slices root ginger,
  shredded
1 teaspoon sesame seed
  oil
freshly ground black
  pepper

AMERICAN

1 lb boneless chicken
  (breasts and thighs),
  cut into small pieces
1½ tablespoons soy
  sauce
1 tablespoon pale dry
  sherry
1 teaspoon sugar
1 teaspoon cornstarch
4 Chinese dried
  mushrooms
1 tablespoon vegetable
  oil
2 slices ginger root,
  shredded
1 teaspoon sesame seed
  oil
freshly ground black
  pepper

Put the chicken in a bowl with the soy sauce, sherry, sugar and cornflour (cornstarch). Mix well and leave to marinate for about 20 minutes.

Soak the mushrooms in warm water for 20 minutes. Squeeze dry and remove the hard stalks. Cut the mushroom caps into pieces roughly the same size as the chicken.

Brush a heatproof plate with the vegetable oil. Place the chicken pieces on the plate, top with the mushrooms, then sprinkle with the ginger, sesame seed oil and pepper to taste.

Place the plate in a steamer or over a pan of simmering water and cover with a lid. Steam over high heat for 25 to 30 minutes. Serve hot.
Serves 4

Meat Dishes

White-Cooked Boiled Pork

METRIC/IMPERIAL
2.5 litres/4½ pints water
1.5 kg/3 lb piece boned
  belly pork
Garnish:
1 chrysanthemum head
  or 1 tomato
Dips:
4 garlic cloves, crushed
2 tablespoons sesame
  seed oil
2 tablespoons soy sauce
1 tablespoon shredded
  root ginger
2 tablespoons hoisin
  sauce

AMERICAN
5½ pints water
3 lb piece fresh pork
  sides
Garnish:
1 chrysanthemum head
  or 1 tomato
Dips:
4 garlic cloves, minced
2 tablespoons sesame
  seed oil
2 tablespoons soy sauce
1 tablespoon shredded
  ginger root
2 tablespoons hoisin
  sauce

Bring the water to the boil in a large saucepan. Add the pork and slowly return to the boil. Skim the surface. Boil steadily for 10 minutes, then turn off the heat and leave for 10 minutes.

Repeat the boiling and resting process twice. Leave the pork to cool in the water.

When cold, drain the pork and cut across the lean and fat into thin slices. Arrange on a serving dish and garnish with the chrysanthemum; or, halve the tomato, making zigzag cuts around the middle, to make two "waterlilies" and place on the pork.

To make the dips, put the garlic and sesame seed oil in one small bowl, the soy sauce and ginger in another, and the hoisin sauce in a third bowl. Serve with the pork.
Serves 8 to 12

Deep-Fried Meatballs

METRIC/IMPERIAL
450 g/1 lb minced pork
1 teaspoon grated root
  ginger
2 tablespoons cornflour
½ teaspoon salt
1 egg
1 tablespoon soy sauce
2 tablespoons plain flour
oil for deep-frying
Garnish:
lemon slices
parsley sprig

AMERICAN
1 lb ground pork
1 teaspoon finely
  chopped ginger root
2 tablespoons
  cornstarch
½ teaspoon salt
1 egg
1 tablespoon soy sauce
2 tablespoons all-
  purpose flour
oil for deep-frying
Garnish:
lemon slices
parsley sprig

Mix all the ingredients together and form into small balls. Heat the oil in a wok or deep-fryer to 180°C/350°F. Deep-fry the meatballs a few at a time, turning frequently, until they float to the surface. Drain and cool slightly.

Reheat the oil to 180°C/350°F. Return the meatballs to the oil and fry for 1 minute to make them extra crispy. Drain on kitchen paper towels.

Arrange on a warmed serving dish and garnish with lemon slices and parsley. Serve hot with hoisin sauce and tomato ketchup.
Serves 4

White-Cooked Boiled Pork with assorted dips

Steamed Spareribs in Black Bean Sauce

METRIC/IMPERIAL	AMERICAN
450 g/1 lb pork spareribs	1 lb pork spareribs
1 garlic clove, crushed	1 garlic clove, minced
1 slice root ginger, finely chopped	1 slice ginger root, finely chopped
1 tablespoon vegetable oil	1 tablespoon vegetable oil
Sauce:	**Sauce:**
2 tablespoons black bean sauce	2 tablespoons salted black beans
1 tablespoon soy sauce	1 tablespoon soy sauce
1 teaspoon sugar	1 teaspoon sugar
1 teaspoon dry sherry	1 teaspoon pale dry sherry
1 teaspoon cornflour	1 teaspoon cornstarch
Garnish:	**Garnish:**
1 small green or red pepper, cored, seeded and shredded	1 small green or red pepper, seeded and shredded
1 teaspoon sesame seed oil (optional)	1 teaspoon sesame seed oil (optional)

Chop the spareribs into small pieces and place in a bowl with the garlic, ginger and sauce ingredients. Mix well and leave to marinate for about 20 minutes.

Brush a heatproof plate with the vegetable oil, then put the sparerib mixture on the plate. Place in a steamer, or over a pan of boiling water, and cover with a lid. Steam over high heat for 30 minutes. Sprinkle with the green or red pepper and sesame seed oil, if using. Serve hot.

Serves 2 to 4

Pork Slices with Cauliflower

METRIC/IMPERIAL	AMERICAN
4 Chinese dried mushrooms	4 Chinese dried mushrooms
225 g/8 oz boned lean pork, sliced	$\frac{1}{2}$ lb pork loin, sliced
2 tablespoons soy sauce	2 tablespoons soy sauce
1 tablespoon dry sherry	1 tablespoon pale dry sherry
1 tablespoon cornflour	1 tablespoon cornstarch
1 cauliflower, broken into florets	1 cauliflower, broken into florets
salt	salt
3 tablespoons vegetable oil	3 tablespoons vegetable oil
2 spring onions, cut into 2.5 cm/1 inch lengths	2 scallions, cut into 1 inch lengths
1 slice root ginger, cut into strips	1 slice ginger root, cut into strips

Soak the mushrooms in warm water for 20 minutes. Squeeze dry, remove the hard stalks, then cut the mushroom caps into halves or quarters, according to size.

Put the pork in a bowl and sprinkle with the soy sauce, sherry and 1 teaspoon of the cornflour (cornstarch). Mix well and leave to marinate for about 20 minutes.

Meanwhile, blanch the cauliflower in boiling salted water for 1 to 2 minutes; drain and set aside.

Heat the oil in a wok or frying pan (skillet). Add the spring onions (scallions) and ginger, then the pork. Stir-fry until the pork is evenly browned, then add the mushrooms and 1 teaspoon salt. Stir-fry for 1 minute, then add the cauliflower and stir well.

Blend the remaining cornflour (cornstarch) with a little water, add to the pan and cook, stirring, until thickened.

Arrange the cauliflower around the edge of a warmed serving dish and pile the pork mixture into the centre. Serve hot.

Serves 2

Sweet and Sour Pork

METRIC/IMPERIAL	AMERICAN
350 g/12 oz pork fillet	¾ lb boneless pork
2 tablespoons dry sherry	tenderloin
salt	2 tablespoons pale dry
freshly ground black	sherry
pepper	salt
1 tablespoon cornflour	freshly ground black
120 ml/4 fl oz water	pepper
1 tablespoon tomato	1 tablespoon cornstarch
ketchup	½ cup water
5 tablespoons sugar	1 tablespoon tomato
1 tablespoon soy sauce	ketchup
2 teaspoons red wine	5 tablespoons sugar
vinegar	1 tablespoon soy sauce
oil for deep-frying	2 teaspoons red wine
3 tablespoons vegetable	vinegar
oil	oil for deep-frying
1 green pepper, cored,	3 tablespoons vegetable
seeded and thinly	oil
sliced	1 green pepper, seeded
½ onion, sliced into rings	and thinly sliced
Batter:	½ onion, sliced into rings
2 egg yolks	**Batter:**
2 tablespoons plain flour	2 egg yolks
2 tablespoons water	2 tablespoons all-
	purpose flour
	2 tablespoons water

Cut the pork into strips. Sprinkle with half of the sherry and a pinch each of salt and pepper.

Mix the cornflour (cornstarch) with a little of the water, then stir in the remainder, together with the tomato ketchup, sugar, soy sauce, vinegar, remaining sherry and 1 teaspoon salt.

Beat together the egg yolks, flour and water to make a smooth batter. Heat the oil in a wok or deep-fryer to 180°C/350°F. Dip the pork into the batter and deep-fry until golden brown. Drain on kitchen paper towels and keep hot.

Heat the 3 tablespoons vegetable oil in a wok or frying pan (skillet). Add the green pepper and onion and stir-fry for 2 minutes. Add the soy sauce mixture and cook, stirring, until thickened. Add the pork and mix well.

Transfer to a warmed serving dish and serve hot.
Serves 2 to 4

Braised Meatballs

METRIC/IMPERIAL	AMERICAN
3 Chinese dried	3 Chinese dried
mushrooms	mushrooms
50 g/2 oz transparent	2 oz cellophane noodles
noodles	1 cup ground pork
225 g/8 oz finely	1 egg white
minced pork	2 tablespoons soy sauce
1 egg white	1 tablespoon pale dry
2 tablespoons soy sauce	sherry
1 tablespoon dry sherry	1 teaspoon sugar
1 teaspoon sugar	1 tablespoon cornstarch
1 tablespoon cornflour	3 tablespoons vegetable
3 tablespoons vegetable	oil
oil	1 slice ginger root, finely
1 slice root ginger, finely	chopped
chopped	2 scallions, white part
2 spring onions, white	only, finely chopped
part only, finely	½ lb Chinese cabbage
chopped	(bok choy), shredded
225 g/8 oz Chinese	1 teaspoon salt
cabbage, shredded	2 cups chicken stock
1 teaspoon salt	(approximately)
450 ml/¾ pint chicken	
stock (approximately)	

Soak the mushrooms in warm water for 20 minutes. Squeeze dry, then remove the hard stalks.

Soak the noodles in warm water for 10 minutes; drain.

Mix the pork with the egg white, soy sauce, sherry, sugar and cornflour (cornstarch). Form the mixture into about 8 meatballs.

Heat the oil in a pan, add the meatballs and fry until golden. Remove with a slotted spoon, drain on kitchen paper towels and keep on one side. Add the ginger and spring onions (scallions) to the pan, then stir in the cabbage, mushrooms and salt. Return the meatballs to the pan and pour in just enough stock to cover. Bring to the boil, then simmer for 25 minutes.

Stir in the noodles and simmer for about 3 minutes. Serve hot.
Serves 4

Stir-Fried Bean Curd with Pork and Cabbage

METRIC/IMPERIAL	AMERICAN
1 cake bean curd	1 cake bean curd
225 g/8 oz lean pork	½ lb pork butt or loin
3 tablespoons vegetable oil	3 tablespoons vegetable oil
1 spring onion, chopped	1 scallion, chopped
2 slices root ginger, chopped	2 slices ginger root, chopped
2 teaspoons salt	2 teaspoons salt
1 tablespoon dry sherry	1 tablespoon pale dry sherry
1 litre/1¾ pints stock	4¼ cups stock
450 g/1 lb Chinese cabbage, shredded	1 lb Chinese cabbage (bok choy), shredded

Cut the bean curd into 3.5 cm/1½ inch squares. Freeze overnight. Thaw in hot water, then drain.

Cut the pork into thin bite-sized pieces.

Heat the oil in a saucepan. Add the pork, spring onion (scallion), ginger and bean curd and stir-fry until the meat is lightly browned. Add the salt, sherry and stock and bring to the boil. Cover and simmer for 10 minutes.

Add the cabbage and simmer until tender, about 10 minutes. Serve hot.

Serves 4 to 6

Note: small holes may be left in the bean curd after thawing; these permit the delicious juices to penetrate the bean curd. Do not freeze for more than 12 hours or it will toughen.

Sautéed Lamb with Spring Onions (Scallions)

METRIC/IMPERIAL	AMERICAN
2 tablespoons soy sauce	2 tablespoons soy sauce
½ teaspoon salt	½ teaspoon salt
1 tablespoon dry sherry	1 tablespoon pale dry sherry
120 ml/4 fl oz vegetable oil	½ cup vegetable oil
225 g/8 oz lean lamb, very thinly sliced	½ lb lean lamb, very thinly sliced
1 tablespoon red wine vinegar	1 tablespoon red wine vinegar
1 tablespoon sesame seed oil	1 tablespoon sesame seed oil
½ teaspoon ground Szechuan or black peppercorns	½ teaspoon ground Szechuan or black peppercorns
2 garlic cloves, crushed	2 garlic cloves, minced
225 g/8 oz spring onions	½ lb scallions (2 bunches)

Mix together 1 tablespoon of the soy sauce, the salt, sherry and 2 tablespoons of the oil. Add the lamb and leave to marinate for 5 minutes.

Mix the remaining soy sauce with the vinegar, sesame seed oil and pepper in a small bowl.

Heat the remaining oil in a wok or frying pan (skillet). Add the garlic and stir-fry for 10 seconds. Add the meat and stir-fry until browned. Shred a few of the spring onions (scallions) and set aside for garnish. Cut the remainder into 5 cm/2 inch pieces and add to the pan with the vinegar mixture. Stir-fry for a few seconds. Serve hot, garnished with the reserved spring onions (scallions).

Serves 2 to 4

Note: beef may be substituted for lamb, if preferred.

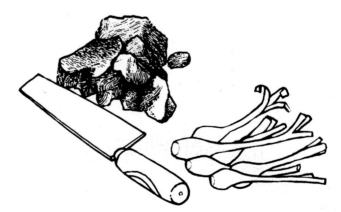

Stir-Fried Bean Curd with Pork and Cabbage (above)
Sautéed Lamb with Spring Onions (Scallions) (below)

Red-Cooked Pork

METRIC/IMPERIAL
4 Chinese dried
  mushrooms
1 leg or shoulder of
  pork, weighing
  1.5 kg/3–3½ lb
1 garlic clove, crushed
6 tablespoons soy sauce
3 tablespoons dry sherry
3 tablespoons
  crystallized or brown
  sugar
1 teaspoon five-spice
  powder

AMERICAN
4 Chinese dried
  mushrooms
1 pork leg or shoulder,
  weighing 3–3½ lb
1 garlic clove, minced
6 tablespoons soy sauce
3 tablespoons pale dry
  sherry
3 tablespoons rock or
  brown sugar
1 teaspoon five-spice
  powder

Soak the mushrooms in warm water for 20 minutes. Squeeze dry and remove the hard stalks.

Put the pork in a large pan of cold water. Bring to the boil, boil for a few minutes, then drain. Rinse the pork under cold running water, then drain again.

Return the pork to the cleaned pan. Add the mushrooms, garlic, soy sauce, sherry, sugar and five-spice powder. Cover with a tight-fitting lid and bring to the boil, then simmer for 2 to 3 hours, turning several times during cooking.

There should be very little liquid left at the end of the cooking time; if necessary, increase the heat and simmer, uncovered, until the liquid has reduced and thickened.

Place the pork on a serving dish and pour over any thickened cooking liquid. Serve hot or cold.
Serves 6

Shredded Pork with Bean Sprouts

METRIC/IMPERIAL
225 g/8 oz bean sprouts
350 g/12 oz boned lean
  pork, shredded
2 tablespoons soy sauce
1 teaspoon dry sherry
2 teaspoons cornflour
3 tablespoons vegetable
  oil
2 spring onions,
  shredded
1 slice root ginger,
  shredded
1 teaspoon salt
50 g/2 oz leeks,
  shredded

AMERICAN
4 cups bean sprouts
1½ cups shredded pork
  loin
2 tablespoons soy sauce
1 teaspoon pale dry
  sherry
2 teaspoons cornstarch
3 tablespoons vegetable
  oil
2 scallions, shredded
1 slice ginger root,
  shredded
1 teaspoon salt
1 small leek, shredded

Rinse the bean sprouts in cold water, discarding any husks that float to the surface. Drain well.

Put the pork in a bowl. Sprinkle with the soy sauce, sherry and cornflour (cornstarch). Mix well and leave to marinate for about 20 minutes.

Heat 1 tablespoon of the oil in a wok or frying pan (skillet). Add the spring onions (scallions) and ginger, then the pork. Stir-fry until the pork is evenly browned, then remove from the pan with a slotted spoon and drain on kitchen paper towels.

Heat the remaining oil in the pan. Add the salt, then the bean sprouts and leeks. Stir-fry for about 1 minute. Return the pork to the pan, stir well and cook for 1 minute. Serve hot.
Serves 4 to 6

Stir-Fried Pork with Bamboo Shoot

METRIC/IMPERIAL	AMERICAN
225 g/8 oz boned lean pork, thinly sliced	1 cup thinly sliced pork loin
1 teaspoon dry sherry	1 teaspoon pale dry sherry
2 tablespoons soy sauce	2 tablespoons soy sauce
3 tablespoons vegetable oil	3 tablespoons vegetable oil
1 garlic clove, chopped	1 garlic clove, chopped
275 g/10 oz canned bamboo shoot, drained and thinly sliced	2½ cups thinly sliced canned bamboo shoot
2 teaspoons vinegar	2 teaspoons vinegar
shredded spring onion and tomato to garnish	shredded scallion and tomato for garnish

Put the pork in a bowl with the sherry and ½ tablespoon of the soy sauce. Mix well and leave to marinate for about 20 minutes.

Heat the oil in a wok or frying pan (skillet), add the garlic and fry until golden brown. Remove from the pan with a slotted spoon and discard.

Add the pork to the pan and stir-fry for 2 minutes. Add the bamboo shoot, the remaining soy sauce and the vinegar. Stir-fry for about 30 seconds. Serve hot, garnished with shredded spring onion (scallion) and tomato.
Serves 4

Spareribs in Sweet and Sour Sauce

METRIC/IMPERIAL	AMERICAN
450 g/1 lb pork spareribs	1 lb pork spareribs
½ teaspoon salt	½ teaspoon salt
1 tablespoon dry sherry	1 tablespoon pale dry sherry
1 teaspoon cornflour	1 teaspoon cornstarch
4 tablespoons vegetable oil	¼ cup vegetable oil
Sauce:	**Sauce:**
50 g/2 oz sugar	¼ cup sugar
3 tablespoons wine vinegar	3 tablespoons wine vinegar
2 tablespoons soy sauce	2 tablespoons soy sauce
1 teaspoon cornflour	1 teaspoon cornstarch

Cut the spareribs into 2.5 cm/1 inch squares. Mix together the salt, sherry and cornflour (cornstarch) in a dish. Add the sparerib pieces, toss to coat with the mixture and leave to marinate for about 30 minutes.

Heat the oil in a wok or frying pan (skillet). Add the sparerib pieces and fry over low heat for about 2 minutes. Remove with a slotted spoon and drain. Increase the heat and when the oil is really hot, return the spareribs to the pan and fry for about 30 seconds until golden. Remove with a slotted spoon and drain on kitchen paper towels. Keep hot.

Mix together the sauce ingredients and add to the pan. When the sauce is bubbling, mix in the spareribs. Stir well until each piece is coated with the sauce. Serve hot.
Serves 2 to 4

Stir-Fried Beef with Onions

METRIC/IMPERIAL	AMERICAN
450 g/1 lb rump steak	1 lb flank steak
1 tablespoon dry sherry	1 tablespoon pale dry sherry
$\frac{1}{2}$ teaspoon salt	$\frac{1}{2}$ teaspoon salt
2 tablespoons soy sauce	2 tablespoons soy sauce
1 teaspoon sugar	1 teaspoon sugar
4 tablespoons vegetable oil	$\frac{1}{4}$ cup vegetable oil
freshly ground black pepper	freshly ground black pepper
2–3 slices root ginger, shredded	2–3 slices ginger root, shredded
1 large onion, thinly sliced	1 large onion, thinly sliced
3 garlic cloves, crushed	3 garlic cloves, minced
1$\frac{1}{2}$ teaspoons cornflour, blended with 3 tablespoons stock	1$\frac{1}{2}$ teaspoons cornstarch, blended with 3 tablespoons stock
Garnish:	**Garnish:**
tomato wedges	tomato wedges
shredded spring onion	shredded scallion

Cut the steak, against the grain, into thin shreds. Mix together the sherry, salt, soy sauce, sugar, 1$\frac{1}{2}$ teaspoons of the oil and pepper to taste in a shallow dish. Add the steak and leave to marinate for 15 minutes.

Heat 2$\frac{1}{4}$ tablespoons of the remaining oil in a wok or frying pan (skillet) over high heat. Add the ginger and onion and stir-fry for 1$\frac{1}{2}$ minutes. Push them to one side and add the remaining oil to the other side of the pan. When it is very hot, add the steak and garlic and stir-fry for a few seconds until brown. Mix in the onion and ginger and stir-fry for 1 minute.

Stir in the blended cornflour (cornstarch) and cook, stirring, for about 30 seconds or until thickened.

Garnish with tomato wedges and shredded spring onion (scallion) to serve.
Serves 4

Double-Stir-Fried Pork in Soy Bean Paste (Sauce)

METRIC/IMPERIAL	AMERICAN
750 g/1$\frac{1}{2}$ lb lean pork	1$\frac{1}{2}$ lb lean pork (loin)
3 tablespoons vegetable oil	3 tablespoons vegetable oil
1 tablespoon hoisin sauce	1 tablespoon hoisin sauce
1 tablespoon dry sherry	1 tablespoon pale dry sherry
1$\frac{1}{2}$ teaspoons soy bean paste	1$\frac{1}{2}$ teaspoons bean sauce
1 tablespoon soy sauce	1 tablespoon soy sauce
1 teaspoon sugar	1 teaspoon sugar
15 g/$\frac{1}{2}$ oz lard	1 tablespoon lard
1 teaspoon cornflour, blended with 3 tablespoons stock or water	1 teaspoon cornstarch, blended with 3 tablespoons stock or water
shredded lettuce to serve (optional)	shredded lettuce to serve (optional)

Cut the pork into 2 cm/$\frac{3}{4}$ inch cubes. Place in a bowl with 1$\frac{1}{2}$ tablespoons of the oil and turn to coat well.

Mix together the hoisin sauce, sherry, soy bean paste (bean sauce), soy sauce and sugar in a bowl.

Heat the remaining oil in a wok or frying pan (skillet) over high heat. Add the pork and stir-fry for 2 minutes. Remove with a slotted spoon, drain on kitchen paper towels and set aside. Discard the cooking oil from the pan.

Melt the lard in the pan, add the soy bean paste (bean sauce) mixture and stir well. Add the blended cornflour (cornstarch) and cook, stirring, until thickened. Return the pork to the pan and stir-fry for 1 minute.

Serve hot on a bed of shredded lettuce, if liked.
Serves 6

Stir-Fried Beef with Onions (above)
Double-Stir-Fried Pork in Soy Bean Paste (Sauce) (below)

Pork Cooked in Barbecue Sauce

METRIC/IMPERIAL	AMERICAN
750 g/1½ lb pork fillet, cut into thick strips	1½ lb pork loin, cut into thick strips
2 tablespoons dry sherry	2 tablespoons pale dry sherry
3 tablespoons sugar	3 tablespoons sugar
2 tablespoons soy sauce	2 tablespoons soy sauce
½ teaspoon five-spice powder	½ teaspoon five-spice powder
1 teaspoon salt	1 teaspoon salt
3 tablespoons vegetable oil	3 tablespoons vegetable oil
2 spring onions, finely chopped	2 scallions, finely chopped
1 slice root ginger, finely chopped	1 slice ginger root, finely chopped
1 garlic clove, finely chopped	1 garlic clove, finely chopped

Put the pork in a bowl with the sherry, sugar, soy sauce, five-spice powder and salt. Mix well and leave to marinate for at least 2 hours, turning occasionally.

Heat the oil in a wok or frying pan (skillet). Add the spring onions (scallions), ginger and garlic and stir-fry for a few seconds.

Drain the pork, reserving the marinade, add to the pan and fry until brown. Remove the pork and vegetables from the pan, pour off the excess oil, then add the reserved marinade and heat through. Return the pork and vegetables to the pan and cook gently until almost all the liquid has been absorbed.

Leave to cool, then cut the pork into thin slices. Serve cold.
Serves 6

Beef and Carrot Stew

METRIC/IMPERIAL	AMERICAN
750 g/1½ lb stewing beef	1½ lb stewing beef
2 tablespoons vegetable oil	2 tablespoons vegetable oil
1 garlic clove, crushed	1 garlic clove, minced
1 slice root ginger, chopped	1 slice ginger root, chopped
1 spring onion, chopped	1 scallion, chopped
4 tablespoons soy sauce	¼ cup soy sauce
1 tablespoon sugar	1 tablespoon sugar
1 tablespoon dry sherry	1 tablespoon pale dry sherry
½ teaspoon five-spice powder	½ teaspoon five-spice powder
450 g/1 lb carrots	1 lb carrots

Cut the beef into 1 cm/½ inch squares.

Heat the oil in a heavy pan or flameproof casserole. Add the garlic, ginger and spring onion (scallion) and fry until golden brown. Add the beef and the remaining ingredients, except the carrots, with just enough cold water to cover. Bring to the boil, cover and simmer for about 1½ hours.

Cut the carrots diagonally into diamond shapes. Add to the beef and simmer for 30 minutes or until the beef and carrots are tender. Serve hot.
Serves 6 to 8

Stir-Fried Beef with Green Peppers

METRIC/IMPERIAL	AMERICAN
225 g/8 oz beef, thinly sliced	1 cup thinly sliced flank or round steak
2 teaspoons salt	2 teaspoons salt
2 teaspoons sugar	2 teaspoons sugar
1 tablespoon dry sherry	1 tablespoon pale dry sherry
1 tablespoon cornflour	1 tablespoon cornstarch
½ teaspoon chilli sauce (optional)	½ teaspoon chili sauce (optional)
freshly ground black pepper	freshly ground black pepper
3 tablespoons vegetable oil	3 tablespoons vegetable oil
1 large green pepper, cored, seeded and thinly sliced	1 large green pepper, seeded and thinly sliced
1 large tomato, cut into 6 pieces	1 large tomato, cut into 6 pieces
2 spring onions, chopped	2 scallions, chopped
1 slice root ginger, finely chopped	1 slice ginger root, finely chopped
1 tablespoon soy sauce	1 tablespoon soy sauce

Put the steak in a bowl with ½ teaspoon of the salt, the sugar, sherry, cornflour (cornstarch), chilli sauce, if using, and pepper to taste. Mix well and leave to marinate for about 20 minutes.

Heat 1 tablespoon of the oil in a wok or frying pan (skillet). Add the green pepper, tomato and remaining salt and stir-fry for a few seconds over high heat. Remove from the pan with a slotted spoon and drain.

Heat the remaining oil in the pan. Add the spring onions (scallions) and ginger, then the meat. Stir-fry for a few seconds, then add the soy sauce. Return the green pepper mixture to the pan and stir well. Serve hot.
Serves 2

Sliced Beef with Bamboo Shoot

METRIC/IMPERIAL	AMERICAN
4 large Chinese dried mushrooms	4 large Chinese dried mushrooms
225 g/8 oz beef (rump or topside), thinly sliced	½ lb flank steak, thinly sliced
2 teaspoons dry sherry	2 teaspoons pale dry sherry
5 teaspoons soy sauce	5 teaspoons soy sauce
1 egg white	1 egg white
1 tablespoon cornflour	1 tablespoon cornstarch
4 tablespoons vegetable oil	¼ cup vegetable oil
100 g/4 oz canned bamboo shoot, drained and thinly sliced	½ cup thinly sliced canned bamboo shoot
½ teaspoon salt	½ teaspoon salt
pinch of freshly ground black pepper	pinch of freshly ground black pepper
1 spring onion, shredded (optional)	1 scallion, shredded (optional)

Soak the mushrooms in warm water for 20 minutes. Squeeze dry, remove the hard stalks and cut the mushroom caps into quarters.

Cut the beef into bite-sized pieces. Combine the sherry, 2 teaspoons of the soy sauce, the egg white and cornflour (cornstarch) in a bowl. Add the beef and toss to coat thoroughly.

Heat the oil in a wok or frying pan (skillet). Add the beef and stir-fry until just brown. Add the bamboo shoot and mushrooms and stir-fry for a few seconds. Stir in the remaining soy sauce, the salt and pepper. Transfer to a warmed serving dish and garnish with the shredded spring onion (scallion) if using.
Serves 2

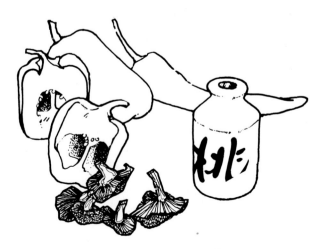

Braised Pork with Pumpkin

METRIC/IMPERIAL	AMERICAN
450 g/1 lb pumpkin	1 lb pumpkin
350 g/12 oz belly pork, skinned	¾ lb fresh pork sides (boneless)
2 tablespoons dry sherry	2 tablespoons pale dry sherry
5 tablespoons soy sauce	⅓ cup soy sauce
3 tablespoons vegetable oil	3 tablespoons vegetable oil
300 ml/½ pint stock or water	1¼ cups stock or water
2 teaspoons sugar	2 teaspoons sugar

Peel the pumpkin, remove the seeds and cut into 5 cm/2 inch cubes. Cut the pork into 1 cm/½ inch thick pieces.

Mix together half the sherry and 1 tablespoon of the soy sauce in a bowl. Add the pork and turn to coat thoroughly.

Heat the oil in a wok or frying pan (skillet), add the pork and stir-fry until evenly browned. Add the pumpkin. Stir well, then add the stock or water, sugar and remaining sherry and soy sauce. Bring to the boil and simmer for 15 minutes, or until the pumpkin is tender. Serve hot.
Serves 4 to 6

Braised Beef with Turnips

METRIC/IMPERIAL	AMERICAN
1.25 kg/2½ lb stewing beef, in 2 pieces	2½ lb beef rump, in 2 pieces
3 slices root ginger	3 slices ginger root
2 whole star anise	2 whole star anise
1 teaspoon Szechuan or black peppercorns	1 teaspoon Szechuan or black peppercorns
120 ml/4 fl oz soy sauce	½ cup soy sauce
1 tablespoon sugar	1 tablespoon sugar
2 tablespoons dry sherry	2 tablespoons pale dry sherry
1 kg/2 lb turnips	2 lb turnips
2 teaspoons cornflour, blended with 2 tablespoons water	2 teaspoons cornstarch, blended with 2 tablespoons water
parsley sprig to garnish	parsley sprig for garnish

Put the beef in a saucepan with the ginger, anise, peppercorns, soy sauce, sugar and sherry. Add enough water just to cover the meat and bring to the boil. Cover and simmer for 1 hour or until tender.

Meanwhile, cut the turnips into 1 cm/½ inch thick slices and parboil for 2 minutes; drain.

Remove the beef from the pan and cut into 1 cm/½ inch thick slices. Put into a deep heatproof bowl and arrange the turnips on top. Pour the liquid from the pan over the turnips and steam for 30 minutes.

Drain the liquid from the bowl into a saucepan, discarding the ginger and anise. Arrange the beef and turnips in a warmed serving dish and keep hot.

Add the blended cornflour (cornstarch) to the pan and simmer, stirring, until thickened. Pour over the beef and turnips. Serve hot, garnished with parsley.
Serves 8

Red-Cooked Beef

METRIC/IMPERIAL	AMERICAN
750 g/1½ lb stewing beef, in one piece	1½ lb stewing beef, in one piece
4 slices root ginger	4 slices ginger root
2 tablespoons dry sherry	2 tablespoons pale dry sherry
2 tablespoons vegetable oil	2 tablespoons vegetable oil
5 tablespoons soy sauce	⅓ cup soy sauce
1 tablespoon sugar	1 tablespoon sugar
1 tablespoon sesame seed oil (optional)	1 tablespoon sesame seed oil (optional)

Put the beef, ginger and sherry in a large pan. Add just enough water to cover and bring to the boil. Skim the surface, cover and simmer for about 1 hour.

Remove the beef from the pan, reserving the cooking liquid, drain and cut into 2.5 cm/1 inch chunks.

Heat the vegetable oil in a clean pan, add the beef and stir-fry for about 30 seconds, then add the soy sauce, sugar and reserved cooking liquid.

Cover and simmer for about 40 minutes or until the beef is tender. Sprinkle with the sesame seed oil, if using. Serve hot.
Serves 6

Braised Pork with Pumpkin (above)
Braised Beef with Turnips (below)

Stir-Fried Beef with Broccoli

METRIC/IMPERIAL
225 g/8 oz lean beef
  steak, thinly sliced
2 teaspoons salt
1 teaspoon dry sherry
1 tablespoon cornflour
4 tablespoons vegetable
  oil
225 g/8 oz broccoli,
  broken into small
  florets
little chicken stock or
  water (optional)
2 spring onions, cut into
  2.5 cm/1 inch lengths
100 g/4 oz button
  mushrooms, sliced
1 tablespoon soy sauce

AMERICAN
½ lb flank or round
  steak, thinly sliced
2 teaspoons salt
1 teaspoon pale dry
  sherry
1 tablespoon cornstarch
¼ cup vegetable oil
½ lb broccoli, broken
  into small florets
little chicken stock or
  water (optional)
2 scallions, cut into
  1 inch lengths
1 cup button
  mushrooms, sliced
1 tablespoon soy sauce

Put the steak in a bowl with ½ teaspoon of the salt, the sherry and cornflour (cornstarch). Mix well and leave to marinate for 20 minutes.

Heat 2 tablespoons of the oil in a wok or frying pan (skillet). Add the broccoli and remaining salt and stir-fry for a few minutes, adding a little stock or water to moisten if necessary. Remove from the pan with a slotted spoon, drain and keep on one side.

Heat the remaining oil in the pan. Add the spring onions (scallions) and fry for a few seconds. Add the steak and stir-fry until evenly browned. Stir in the mushrooms, soy sauce and broccoli. Serve hot.
Serves 4

Sautéed Beef with Mushrooms

METRIC/IMPERIAL
50 g/2 oz Chinese dried
  mushrooms
1 egg white
2½ tablespoons soy
  sauce
1 teaspoon cornflour
450 g/1 lb lean beef,
  shredded
7 tablespoons vegetable
  oil
100 g/4 oz canned
  bamboo shoot,
  drained and shredded
1 tablespoon red wine
1 teaspoon sugar
½ teaspoon salt

AMERICAN
1 cup Chinese dried
  mushrooms
1 egg white
2½ tablespoons soy
  sauce
1 teaspoon cornstarch
1 lb flank steak,
  shredded
7 tablespoons vegetable
  oil
1 cup shredded canned
  bamboo shoot
1 tablespoon red wine
1 teaspoon sugar
½ teaspoon salt

Soak the mushrooms in warm water for 20 minutes. Squeeze dry, remove the hard stalks and shred the mushroom caps.

Mix together the egg white, 1 tablespoon of the soy sauce and the cornflour (cornstarch) in a bowl. Add the beef and leave to marinate for 5 minutes.

Heat 4 tablespoons of the oil in a wok or frying pan (skillet). Add the beef and stir-fry over high heat until browned. Remove from the pan with a slotted spoon and set aside.

Heat the remaining oil in the pan. Add the bamboo shoot and mushrooms and stir-fry over high heat until well coated with oil. Return the beef to the pan with the remaining ingredients. Stir-fry for 1 minute. Serve hot.
Serves 4

Beef and Mange-Tout (Snow Peas)

METRIC/IMPERIAL
225 g/8 oz beef steak,
  thinly sliced
2 tablespoons oyster
  sauce
1 tablespoon dry sherry
1 teaspoon cornflour
4 tablespoons vegetable
  oil
2 spring onions, cut into
  2.5 cm/1 inch lengths
1 slice root ginger, cut
  into strips
225 g/8 oz mange-tout,
  topped and tailed
1 tablespoon salt
1 teaspoon sugar

AMERICAN
1 cup thinly sliced flank
  or round steak
2 tablespoons oyster
  sauce
1 tablespoon pale dry
  sherry
1 teaspoon cornstarch
¼ cup vegetable oil
2 scallions, cut into
  1 inch lengths
1 slice ginger root, cut
  into strips
½ lb snow peas, topped
  and tailed
1 tablespoon salt
1 teaspoon sugar

Put the beef in a bowl with the oyster sauce, sherry and cornflour (cornstarch). Mix well and leave to marinate for about 20 minutes.

Heat half the oil in a wok or frying pan (skillet). Add the spring onions (scallions) and ginger. Stir-fry for a few seconds, then add the beef and stir-fry for about 2 minutes, until evenly browned. Transfer to a warmed serving dish and keep hot.

Heat the remaining oil in the pan. Add the mange-tout (snow peas), salt and sugar and stir-fry for about 2 minutes; do not overcook, or the mange-tout (snow peas) will lose their texture and colour.

Add the mange-tout (snow peas) to the beef and mix well. Serve hot.
Serves 4

Fried Lamb Slices with Onions

METRIC/IMPERIAL
225 g/8 oz lean boned
  lamb, thinly sliced
½ teaspoon salt
1 teaspoon cornflour
4 tablespoons vegetable
  oil
225 g/8 oz onions,
  sliced
2 garlic cloves, crushed
2 tablespoons soy sauce
1 tablespoon dry sherry
pinch of monosodium
  glutamate (optional)
1 teaspoon sesame seed
  oil (optional)

AMERICAN
½ lb lean boneless lamb,
  thinly sliced
½ teaspoon salt
1 teaspoon cornstarch
¼ cup vegetable oil
2 onions, sliced
2 garlic cloves, minced
2 tablespoons soy sauce
1 tablespoon pale dry
  sherry
pinch of msg (optional)
1 teaspoon sesame seed
  oil (optional)

Mix the lamb slices with the salt and cornflour (cornstarch). Heat the oil in a wok or frying pan (skillet). When it is very hot, add the lamb and stir-fry until lightly browned. Remove from the pan with a slotted spoon and set aside.

Add the onions and garlic to the pan and fry until just tender. Return the lamb to the pan with the soy sauce, sherry and monosodium glutamate (msg), if using. Stir well. Add the sesame seed oil, if using, just before serving. Serve hot.
Serves 2 to 4

Spiced Leg of Lamb

METRIC/IMPERIAL
1 leg of lamb, weighing
  1.75–2.25 kg/4–5 lb
Sauce:
6 garlic cloves, crushed
6 slices root ginger,
  shredded
2 onions, thinly sliced
1.2 litres/2 pints stock
5 tablespoons soy sauce
3 tablespoons soy bean
  paste or hoisin sauce
2 teaspoons dried chilli
  pepper or chilli sauce
½ teaspoon five-spice
  powder
2 tablespoons sugar
300 ml/½ pint red wine
1 chicken stock cube

AMERICAN
1 leg of lamb, weighing
  4–5 lb
Sauce:
6 garlic cloves, minced
6 slices ginger root,
  shredded
2 onions, thinly sliced
5 cups stock
⅓ cup soy sauce
3 tablespoons bean
  sauce or hoisin sauce
2 teaspoons dried chili
  pepper or chili sauce
½ teaspoon five-spice
  powder
2 tablespoons sugar
1¼ cups red wine
2 chicken bouillon
  cubes

Place the sauce ingredients in a saucepan and mix together. Bring to the boil and simmer for 45 minutes.

Put the leg of lamb in another large saucepan or flameproof casserole. Pour over the sauce. Bring to the boil, cover and simmer for 1½ hours, turning every 30 minutes. Remove from the heat and allow to cool in the sauce, then leave to marinate for a further 3 hours (or overnight).

Place the lamb in a roasting pan and cook in a preheated moderate oven (180°C/350°F, Gas Mark 4) for 1 hour.

Slice the lamb into large bite-sized pieces. Serve hot or cold with dips such as hoisin sauce, soy sauce and sherry mixed together, or soy sauce and vinegar mixed together.
Serves 8

Red-Cooked Lamb

METRIC/IMPERIAL
1 kg/2 lb stewing lamb
4 tablespoons dry sherry
4 slices root ginger
2 garlic cloves, crushed
½ teaspoon five-spice
  powder
stock or water
4 tablespoons soy sauce
1 tablespoon sugar

AMERICAN
2 lb stewing lamb
¼ cup pale dry sherry
4 slices ginger root
2 garlic cloves, minced
½ teaspoon five-spice
  powder
stock or water
¼ cup soy sauce
1 tablespoon sugar

Blanch the lamb in boiling water for 3 minutes. Drain and cut into small cubes. Put in a large pan with the sherry, ginger, garlic and five-spice powder. Cook, stirring, for 2 minutes, then add enough stock or water just to cover the meat. Bring to the boil and simmer for about 1 hour.

Add the soy sauce and sugar and continue cooking for 20 to 30 minutes, or until the sauce is reduced almost to nothing. Serve hot.
Serves 4

Pork and Aubergine (Eggplant) in Hot Sauce

METRIC/IMPERIAL
175 g/6 oz boned lean
  pork, shredded
2 spring onions, finely
  chopped
1 slice root ginger,
  finely chopped
1 garlic clove, finely
  chopped
1 tablespoon soy sauce
1 teaspoon dry sherry
1½ teaspoons cornflour
600 ml/1 pint oil for
  deep-frying
225 g/8 oz aubergine,
  cut into diamond-
  shaped chunks
1 tablespoon chilli sauce
3–4 tablespoons
  chicken stock or
  water
chopped spring onion to
  garnish

AMERICAN
¾ cup shredded pork
  loin
2 scallions, finely
  chopped
1 slice ginger root, finely
  chopped
1 garlic clove, finely
  chopped
1 tablespoon soy sauce
1 teaspoon pale dry
  sherry
1½ teaspoons cornstarch
2½ cups oil for deep-
  frying
½ lb eggplant, cut into
  diamond-shaped
  chunks
1 tablespoon chili sauce
3–4 tablespoons
  chicken stock or
  water
chopped scallion for
  garnish

Put the pork in a bowl with the spring onions (scallions), ginger, garlic, soy sauce, sherry and cornflour (cornstarch). Mix well and leave to marinate for about 20 minutes.

Heat the oil in a wok or deep-fryer to 180°C/350°F. Lower the heat, add the aubergine (eggplant) and deep-fry for about 1½ minutes. Remove from the pan with a slotted spoon and drain on kitchen paper towels.

Pour off all but 1 tablespoon oil from the pan, then add the pork and stir-fry for about 1 minute. Add the aubergine (eggplant) and chilli sauce and cook for about 1½ minutes. Moisten with the stock or water and simmer until the liquid has almost completely evaporated.

Serve hot, garnished with chopped spring onion (scallion).
Serves 2

Stir-Fried Liver with Spinach

METRIC/IMPERIAL
450 g/1 lb spinach
350 g/12 oz pigs' liver,
  cut into thin triangular
  slices
2 tablespoons cornflour
4 tablespoons vegetable
  oil
1 teaspoon salt
2 slices root ginger
1 tablespoon soy sauce
1 tablespoon dry sherry
shredded spring onion
  to garnish

AMERICAN
1 lb spinach
¾ lb pork liver, cut into
  thin triangular slices
2 tablespoons cornstarch
¼ cup vegetable oil
1 teaspoon salt
2 slices ginger root
1 tablespoon soy sauce
1 tablespoon pale dry
  sherry
shredded scallion for
  garnish

Wash and thoroughly drain the spinach.

Blanch the liver for a few seconds in boiling water, drain and coat with the cornflour (cornstarch).

Heat 2 tablespoons of the oil in a wok or frying pan (skillet). Add the spinach and salt and stir-fry for 2 minutes. Remove from the pan, arrange around the edge of a warmed serving dish and keep hot.

Heat the remaining oil in the pan until it reaches smoking point. Add the ginger, liver, soy sauce and sherry. Stir-fry for about 1 minute, until the liver is evenly browned, then pour over the spinach.

Serve immediately, garnished with shredded spring onion (scallion).
Serves 2 to 4

Pork and Aubergine (Eggplant) in Hot Sauce (above)
Stir-Fried Liver with Spinach (below)

Shredded Lamb with Noodles and Spring Onions (Scallions)

METRIC/IMPERIAL	AMERICAN
100 g/4 oz transparent noodles	$\frac{1}{4}$ lb cellophane noodles
1 egg	1 egg
1 tablespoon cornflour	1 tablespoon cornstarch
1$\frac{1}{2}$ tablespoons water	1$\frac{1}{2}$ tablespoons water
225 g/8 oz lean lamb, shredded	$\frac{1}{2}$ lb lean lamb, shredded
3 tablespoons vegetable oil `	3 tablespoons vegetable oil
2 tablespoons soy sauce	2 tablespoons soy sauce
4–5 spring onions, cut into 5 cm/2 inch pieces	4–5 scallions, cut into 2 inch pieces
300 ml/$\frac{1}{2}$ pint chicken stock	1$\frac{1}{4}$ cups chicken stock
1 tablespoon sesame seed oil	1 tablespoon sesame seed oil
2 tablespoons dry sherry	2 tablespoons pale dry sherry

Soak the noodles in hot water for 5 minutes; drain.

Beat the egg with the cornflour (cornstarch) and water. Add the lamb and turn to coat.

Heat the oil in a pan over high heat. Add the lamb and stir-fry for 1 minute. Sprinkle in the soy sauce and spring onions (scallions) and stir-fry for 1 minute. Add the stock and noodles and bring to the boil, stirring. Simmer for 5 minutes.

Sprinkle with the sesame seed oil and sherry and simmer for 1 minute. Serve hot.

Serves 2 to 4

Stir-Fried Kidney Flowers

METRIC/IMPERIAL	AMERICAN
15 g/$\frac{1}{2}$ oz dried wood ears	$\frac{1}{2}$ cup dried tree ears
225 g/8 oz pigs' kidneys	$\frac{1}{2}$ lb pork kidneys
1$\frac{1}{2}$ teaspoons salt	1$\frac{1}{2}$ teaspoons salt
2 teaspoons cornflour	2 teaspoons cornstarch
100 g/4 oz seasonal green vegetables (lettuce, cabbage or spinach)	$\frac{1}{4}$ lb seasonal green vegetables (lettuce, cabbage or spinach)
6 tablespoons vegetable oil	6 tablespoons vegetable oil
1 garlic clove, crushed	1 garlic clove, minced
1 slice root ginger, finely chopped	1 slice ginger root, finely chopped
1 spring onion, finely chopped	1 scallion, finely chopped
50 g/2 oz canned water chestnuts, drained and sliced	$\frac{1}{4}$ cup canned water chestnuts, sliced
50 g/2 oz canned bamboo shoot, drained and sliced	$\frac{1}{2}$ cup sliced canned bamboo shoot
1 tablespoon vinegar	1 tablespoon vinegar
1 tablespoon soy sauce	1 tablespoon soy sauce

Soak the wood (tree) ears in warm water for 20 minutes. Drain and remove the hard parts.

Split the kidneys in half lengthwise and discard the fat and white core. Score the surface of the kidneys in a criss-cross pattern, then cut into pieces. Sprinkle with $\frac{1}{2}$ teaspoon of the salt and 1 teaspoon of the cornflour (cornstarch).

Blanch the green vegetables in boiling water for 1 minute, then drain well.

Heat the oil in a wok or deep pan until it reaches smoking point. Add the kidneys and stir-fry until evenly browned. Remove from the pan with a slotted spoon, drain on kitchen paper towels and keep on one side.

Pour off all but 2 tablespoons oil, then add the garlic, ginger and spring onion (scallion) to the pan. Stir-fry for a few seconds, then add the wood (tree) ears, water chestnuts, bamboo shoot and green vegetables.

Stir in the vinegar and remaining salt, then return the kidneys to the pan. Mix the remaining cornflour (cornstarch) with a little water, add to the pan with the soy sauce and cook, stirring, for 1 minute. Serve hot.

Serves 2 to 4

Stir-Fried Liver with Spring Onions (Scallions)

METRIC/IMPERIAL	AMERICAN
50 g/2 oz dried wood ears	2 cups dried tree ears
350 g/12 oz calves' or lambs' liver, cut into 5 mm/¼ inch thick slices	¾ lb veal or lamb liver, cut into ¼ inch thick slices
7 tablespoons vegetable oil	7 tablespoons vegetable oil
6 spring onions, cut into 5 cm/2 inch pieces	6 scallions, cut into 2 inch pieces
2 slices root ginger	2 slices ginger root
2 tablespoons soy sauce	2 tablespoons soy sauce
1 teaspoon sugar	1 teaspoon sugar
1 tablespoon red wine vinegar	1 tablespoon red wine vinegar
1 tablespoon dry sherry	1 tablespoon pale dry sherry
1 tablespoon cornflour, blended with 250 ml/8 fl oz water	1 tablespoon cornstarch, blended with 1 cup water

Marinade:

½ teaspoon salt	½ teaspoon salt
½ teaspoon freshly ground black pepper	½ teaspoon freshly ground black pepper
2 teaspoons dry sherry	2 teaspoons pale dry sherry
2 teaspoons cornflour	2 teaspoons cornstarch
2 teaspoons vegetable oil	2 teaspoons vegetable oil

Soak the wood (tree) ears in warm water for 20 minutes. Drain and remove the hard stalks.

Soak the liver in cold water for 30 minutes. Drain on kitchen paper towels. Mix the ingredients for the marinade in a bowl. Add the liver slices and leave to marinate for 10 minutes.

Heat 5 tablespoons of the oil in a wok or frying pan (skillet) over high heat. Add the liver and stir-fry rapidly until lightly browned. Transfer to a plate and set aside.

Heat the remaining oil in the pan, add the spring onions (scallions), ginger and wood (tree) ears and stir-fry for 1 minute. Add the soy sauce, sugar, vinegar and sherry and bring to the boil. Return the liver to the pan. Add the blended cornflour (cornstarch) and simmer, stirring, until thickened. Serve hot.
Serves 2 to 4

Sweet and Sour Kidneys

METRIC/IMPERIAL	AMERICAN
750 g/1½ lb pigs' kidneys, thinly sliced	1½ lb pork kidneys, thinly sliced
1 tablespoon dry sherry	1 tablespoon pale dry sherry
2 tablespoons soy sauce	2 tablespoons soy sauce
2 tablespoons red wine vinegar	2 tablespoons red wine vinegar
1 tablespoon sugar	1 tablespoon sugar
4 tablespoons vegetable oil	¼ cup vegetable oil
2 tablespoons chopped spring onions	2 tablespoons chopped scallions
1 teaspoon grated root ginger	1 teaspoon finely chopped ginger root
175 g/6 oz mange-tout or shelled green peas	1 cup snow peas or podded green peas
1 teaspoon cornflour, blended with 1 tablespoon water	1 teaspoon cornstarch, blended with 1 tablespoon water

Soak the kidney slices in cold water for 30 minutes. Drain and parboil in boiling water for 5 minutes. Drain and cool under cold running water. Drain well.

Mix together the sherry, soy sauce, vinegar and sugar in a small bowl.

Heat the oil in a wok or frying pan (skillet) and add the spring onions (scallions) and ginger. Stir-fry for 1 minute, then add the kidney and mange-tout (snow peas) or peas. Stir-fry for a few seconds, then stir in the sherry mixture. Add the blended cornflour (cornstarch) and simmer, stirring constantly, until thickened. Serve hot.
Serves 6

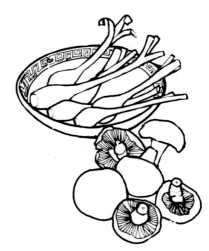

Vegetable & Salad Dishes

Stir-Fried Mixed Vegetables

METRIC/IMPERIAL	AMERICAN
3½ tablespoons vegetable oil	3½ tablespoons vegetable oil
1 onion, thinly sliced	1 onion, thinly sliced
3 garlic cloves, crushed	3 garlic cloves, minced
1½ teaspoons salt	1½ teaspoons salt
½ green pepper, cored, seeded and sliced	½ green pepper, seeded and sliced
½ red pepper, cored, seeded and sliced	½ red pepper, seeded and sliced
¼ cucumber, chopped	¼ cucumber, chopped
2 sticks celery, chopped	2 stalks celery, chopped
2 spring onions, chopped	2 scallions, chopped
3–4 lettuce leaves, chopped	3–4 lettuce leaves, chopped
225 g/8 oz bean sprouts	1⅓ cups bean sprouts
1½ teaspoons sugar	1½ teaspoons sugar
2 tablespoons soy sauce	2 tablespoons soy sauce
2 tablespoons chicken stock	2 tablespoons chicken stock

Heat the oil in a wok or frying pan (skillet), add the onion, garlic and salt and stir-fry for 30 seconds. Add all the other vegetables and toss until well coated.

Sprinkle in the sugar, soy sauce and chicken stock. Stir-fry for 1½ minutes. Serve hot.
Serves 2 to 4

Sweet and Sour Cabbage

METRIC/IMPERIAL	AMERICAN
1 Chinese or Savoy cabbage	1 Chinese cabbage (bok choy) or Savoy cabbage
3 tablespoons vegetable oil	3 tablespoons vegetable oil
15 g/½ oz butter	1 tablespoon butter
1 teaspoon salt	1 teaspoon salt
Sauce:	**Sauce:**
1½ tablespoons cornflour	1½ tablespoons cornstarch
5 tablespoons water	⅓ cup water
1½ tablespoons soy sauce	1½ tablespoons soy sauce
2½ tablespoons sugar	2½ tablespoons sugar
3½ tablespoons vinegar	3½ tablespoons vinegar
3½ tablespoons orange juice	3½ tablespoons orange juice
2½ tablespoons tomato purée	2½ tablespoons tomato paste
1½ tablespoons dry sherry	1½ tablespoons pale dry sherry

Core and shred the cabbage. Heat the oil and butter in a wok or frying pan (skillet). Add the cabbage and sprinkle with the salt. Stir-fry for 2 minutes. Lower the heat and simmer for 5 to 6 minutes.

Mix the sauce ingredients together in a small pan. Bring to the boil and simmer for 4 to 5 minutes, stirring constantly, until the sauce thickens and becomes translucent.

Transfer the cabbage to a warmed serving dish and pour over the sauce. Serve hot.
Serves 4

Stir-Fried Mixed Vegetables

Quick-Fried Beans in Onion and Garlic Sauce

METRIC/IMPERIAL
150 ml/¼ pint chicken
  stock
450 g/1 lb French beans
3 tablespoons vegetable
  oil
25 g/1 oz butter
4–6 garlic cloves,
  crushed
2 spring onions, sliced
1 teaspoon salt
1 tablespoon soy sauce
1 teaspoon sugar
1 tablespoon dry sherry

AMERICAN
⅔ cup chicken stock
1 lb green beans
3 tablespoons vegetable
  oil
2 tablespoons butter
4–6 garlic cloves,
  minced
2 scallions, sliced
1 teaspoon salt
1 tablespoon soy sauce
1 teaspoon sugar
1 tablespoon pale dry
  sherry

Bring the stock to the boil in a large saucepan. Add the beans and simmer until nearly all the liquid has evaporated, turning them constantly.

Heat the oil and butter in a wok or frying pan (skillet), add the garlic, spring onions (scallions) and salt and stir-fry for 30 seconds. Add the beans and toss in the fat until well coated.

Sprinkle with the soy sauce, sugar and sherry and stir-fry for 1 minute. Serve hot with rice and meat dishes.
Serves 4

Cauliflower Fu-Yung

METRIC/IMPERIAL
150 ml/¼ pint chicken
  stock or water
1 large cauliflower,
  broken into very small
  florets
3 egg whites
3–4 tablespoons minced
  chicken breast
1 teaspoon salt
2 tablespoons milk
2 tablespoons cornflour
freshly ground black
  pepper
2 tablespoons vegetable
  oil
25 g/1 oz butter

AMERICAN
⅔ cup chicken stock or
  water
1 large cauliflower,
  broken into very small
  florets
3 egg whites
3–4 tablespoons ground
  chicken breast
1 teaspoon salt
2 tablespoons milk
2 tablespoons
  cornstarch
freshly ground black
  pepper
2 tablespoons vegetable
  oil
2 tablespoons butter

Bring the stock to the boil in a large saucepan, add the cauliflower and cook, stirring, for 3 to 4 minutes, until the liquid has almost evaporated.

Beat the egg whites, chicken, salt, milk, cornflour (cornstarch) and pepper to taste together until the mixture is nearly stiff but not dry.

Heat the oil and butter in a wok or frying pan (skillet), add the egg white mixture and cook, stirring, for 1 minute. Add the cauliflower, increase the heat to high and cook, stirring, for 1½ to 2 minutes, until well covered in the egg white mixture. Turn onto a warmed serving dish and serve at once.
Serves 4

Soy-Braised Cabbage

METRIC/IMPERIAL
1 medium cabbage
*½ chicken stock cube
  dissolved in 5–6
  tablespoons hot water*
2 tablespoons soy sauce
1½ teaspoons sugar
*freshly ground black
  pepper*
*2½ tablespoons
  vegetable oil*
25 g/1 oz lard or butter

AMERICAN
*1 medium-sized
  cabbage*
*1 chicken bouillon cube
  dissolved in 5–6
  tablespoons hot water*
2 tablespoons soy sauce
1½ teaspoons sugar
*freshly ground black
  pepper*
*2½ tablespoons
  vegetable oil*
*2 tablespoons lard or
  butter*

Cut the cabbage into 2.5 cm/1 inch slices, discarding the tougher parts of the stalk. Combine the chicken stock, soy sauce, sugar, and pepper to taste.

Heat the oil and fat in a saucepan, add the cabbage and stir until it is well coated. Sprinkle the soy sauce mixture evenly over the cabbage and stir well. Reduce the heat to very low, cover and simmer for about 20 minutes, stirring every 5 minutes, until tender but still crisp.

Turn into a warmed serving dish and serve at once.
Serves 4

Quick-Fried Spinach

METRIC/IMPERIAL
450 g/1 lb spinach
*3 tablespoons vegetable
  oil*
2 tablespoons butter
1 teaspoon salt
*3–4 garlic cloves,
  crushed*
1 tablespoon soy sauce
1 teaspoon sugar
1 tablespoon dry sherry
15 g/½ oz lard

AMERICAN
1 lb spinach
*3 tablespoons vegetable
  oil*
2 tablespoons butter
1 teaspoon salt
*3–4 garlic cloves,
  minced*
1 tablespoon soy sauce
1 teaspoon sugar
*1 tablespoon pale dry
  sherry*
1 tablespoon lard

Clean, trim and thoroughly dry the spinach.

Heat the oil and butter in a large saucepan. Add the salt and garlic and stir-fry for 30 seconds. Add the spinach and increase the heat to high. Cook, stirring, for 2 minutes, until every leaf is well coated with fat. Sprinkle with the soy sauce, sugar and sherry and stir-fry for 1 minute. Add the lard and stir-fry in the melting fat a few times, to give the spinach a final 'gloss'.

Turn into a warmed serving dish and serve at once.
Serves 4

Aubergines (Eggplants) with Garlic Sauce

METRIC/IMPERIAL	AMERICAN
1 kg/2 lb aubergines	2 lb eggplants
oil for deep-frying	oil for deep-frying
2 tablespoons vegetable oil	2 tablespoons vegetable oil
1 teaspoon crushed garlic	1 teaspoon minced garlic
100 g/4 oz minced pork or beef	½ cup ground pork or beef
½ teaspoon salt	½ teaspoon salt
2 teaspoons sugar	2 teaspoons sugar
2 tablespoons soy sauce	2 tablespoons soy sauce
250 ml/8 fl oz stock or water	1 cup stock or water
2 teaspoons red wine vinegar	2 teaspoons red wine vinegar
1 tablespoon chopped spring onion	1 tablespoon chopped scallion

Peel the aubergines (eggplants) and cut into 2.5 cm/1 inch cubes.

Heat the oil in a wok or deep-fryer to 180°C/350°F. Deep-fry the aubergine (eggplant) cubes until soft. Drain on kitchen paper towels.

Heat the 2 tablespoons vegetable oil in a wok or frying pan (skillet). Add the garlic and meat and stir-fry for a few seconds. Add the salt, sugar, soy sauce and stock or water and bring to the boil. Add the aubergine (eggplant) and cook for 1 minute. Stir in the vinegar and spring onion (scallion). Serve hot.
Serves 6

Dry-Cooked Green Beans

METRIC/IMPERIAL	AMERICAN
oil for deep-frying	oil for deep-frying
450 g/1 lb runner beans	1 lb string beans
2 tablespoons vegetable oil	2 tablespoons vegetable oil
100 g/4 oz minced beef or pork	½ cup ground beef or pork
1 teaspoon salt	1 teaspoon salt
1 teaspoon finely chopped root ginger	1 teaspoon finely chopped ginger root
1 tablespoon sugar	1 tablespoon sugar
5 tablespoons water	⅓ cup water
1 tablespoon soy sauce	1 tablespoon soy sauce

Heat the oil in a wok or deep-fryer to 180°C/350°F. Deep-fry the beans until they are wrinkled. Drain on kitchen paper towels then arrange in a warmed serving dish and keep hot.

Heat the 2 tablespoons vegetable oil in a wok or frying pan (skillet). Add the meat, salt, ginger, sugar, water and soy sauce and stir-fry until the meat begins to brown. Cook over a high heat until all the liquid in the sauce has completely evaporated. Pour over the beans and serve hot.
Serves 4

Aubergine (Eggplant) Salad

METRIC/IMPERIAL	AMERICAN
100 g/4 oz dried shrimps	1½ cups dried shrimp
750 g/1½ lb aubergines	1½ lb eggplants
2 tablespoons vegetable oil	2 tablespoons vegetable oil
4 tablespoons sesame seed paste	¼ cup sesame seed paste
4 tablespoons water	¼ cup water
4 tablespoons chopped spring onions	¼ cup chopped scallions
1 garlic clove, crushed (optional)	1 garlic clove, minced (optional)
3 tablespoons soy sauce	3 tablespoons soy sauce
2 tablespoons red wine vinegar	2 tablespoons red wine vinegar
1 teaspoon sugar	1 teaspoon sugar

Soak the shrimps in warm water for 15 minutes; drain well and chop finely.

Peel the skin from the aubergines (eggplants) then soak in cold water for 5 minutes to prevent discolouration; drain. Steam for about 20 minutes or until just tender. Cut each one lengthwise into quarters and arrange on a plate. Allow to cool, then chill.

Heat the oil in a wok or frying pan (skillet), add the shrimps and stir-fry for 1 minute. Remove from the heat and cool.

Gradually mix the sesame seed paste with the water, then add the shrimps, spring onions (scallions), garlic, if using, soy sauce, vinegar and sugar. Mix well. Pour on top of the chilled aubergine (eggplant). Serve cold.
Serves 6
Note: the aubergines (eggplants) may be baked in the oven rather than steamed. Grated sesame seeds mixed with oil or peanut butter can be used instead of the sesame seed paste.

Aubergines (Eggplants) with Garlic Sauce (above)
Dry-Cooked Green Beans (below)

Chinese Cabbage Salad

METRIC/IMPERIAL	AMERICAN
225 g/8 oz Chinese cabbage or hard white cabbage	½ lb Chinese cabbage (bok choy) or hard white cabbage
Dressing:	**Dressing:**
2 tablespoons soy sauce	2 tablespoons soy sauce
pinch of salt	pinch of salt
1 tablespoon sugar	1 tablespoon sugar
1 tablespoon sesame seed oil	1 tablespoon sesame seed oil

Core and shred the cabbage. Blanch in boiling water for 2 to 3 minutes. Drain and place in a serving bowl.

Mix together the dressing ingredients, pour over the cabbage and toss well. Serve hot or cold.
Serves 2

Shredded Duck Salad

METRIC/IMPERIAL	AMERICAN
2 tablespoons red wine vinegar	2 tablespoons red wine vinegar
2 tablespoons sugar	2 tablespoons sugar
2 tablespoons sesame seed oil	2 tablespoons sesame seed oil
2 tablespoons soy sauce	2 tablespoons soy sauce
1 teaspoon made mustard	1 teaspoon prepared mustard
½ teaspoon salt	½ teaspoon salt
100 g/4 oz carrots, shredded	1 cup shredded carrot
100 g/4 oz cucumber, peeled and shredded	1 cup peeled and shredded cucumber
75 g/3 oz cabbage or Chinese cabbage, cored and shredded	1 cup shredded cabbage or Chinese cabbage (bok choy)
450 g/1 lb roast duck or chicken meat, shredded	1 lb roast duck or chicken meat, shredded

Combine the vinegar, sugar, sesame seed oil, soy sauce, mustard and salt in a bowl; mix thoroughly. Arrange the vegetables on a serving plate. Put the shredded duck or chicken on top. Pour over the dressing just before serving.
Serves 4

Bean Sprout Salad

METRIC/IMPERIAL	AMERICAN
450 g/1 lb bean sprouts	1 lb bean sprouts
salt	salt
2 eggs	2 eggs
1 tablespoon vegetable oil	1 tablespoon vegetable oil
100 g/4 oz cooked ham, cut into thin strips	½ cup thinly sliced cooked ham
Sauce:	**Sauce:**
2 tablespoons soy sauce	2 tablespoons soy sauce
2 tablespoons vinegar	2 tablespoons vinegar
1 tablespoon sesame seed oil	1 tablespoon sesame seed oil
freshly ground black pepper	freshly ground black pepper

Wash and rinse the bean sprouts in cold water, discarding any husks that float to the surface. Cook in boiling salted water for 3 minutes. Drain, rinse in cold water, drain again and set aside.

Beat the eggs with a little salt. Heat the oil in a frying pan (skillet) over a low heat. Add the eggs and cook to make a thin omelet. Remove from the pan, leave to cool, then cut into thin strips.

Combine all the sauce ingredients together, with pepper to taste, and mix with the bean sprouts. Transfer to a serving plate and arrange the ham and omelet strips on top.
Serves 4

Pickled Salad

METRIC/IMPERIAL
2 cucumbers, peeled
450 g/1 lb cabbage,
  cored and chopped
2 teaspoons salt
1 teaspoon crushed
  garlic
1 teaspoon ground
  Szechuan or black
  peppercorns
1 teaspoon sugar
1 tablespoon soy sauce
2 tablespoons sesame
  seed oil
1 tablespoon red wine
  vinegar
few cabbage leaves to
  serve

AMERICAN
2 cucumbers, peeled
1 lb cabbage, cored and
  chopped
2 teaspoons salt
1 teaspoon minced
  garlic
1 teaspoon ground
  Szechuan or black
  peppercorns
1 teaspoon sugar
1 tablespoon soy sauce
2 tablespoons sesame
  seed oil
1 tablespoon red wine
  vinegar
few cabbage leaves to
  serve

Crush the cucumbers until cracks appear on the surface. Quarter lengthwise, then cut into pieces. Place in a bowl with the cabbage, sprinkle with the salt and leave for 2 hours.

Rinse the vegetables under cold running water and drain well on kitchen paper towels. Place in a bowl.

Mix together the garlic, pepper, sugar, soy sauce, oil and vinegar. Pour this mixture over the vegetables and leave to stand for at least 3 hours.

Arrange on a bed of cabbage to serve.
Serves 6 to 8

Spinach Salad

METRIC/IMPERIAL
750 g/1½ lb spinach
2 tablespoons sesame
  seed oil
1 teaspoon sugar
2 tablespoons red wine
  vinegar
3 tablespoons soy sauce
1 teaspoon made
  mustard

AMERICAN
1½ lb spinach
2 tablespoons sesame
  seed oil
1 teaspoon sugar
2 tablespoons red wine
  vinegar
3 tablespoons soy sauce
1 teaspoon prepared
  mustard

Place the spinach in a pan with just the water clinging to the leaves after washing and cook until just tender. Drain well, then refresh under cold running water. Drain again, squeezing out all the water. Cut each leaf into 3 or 4 pieces and place in a serving bowl. Leave to cool.

Combine the sesame seed oil, sugar, vinegar, soy sauce and mustard in a bowl. Pour over the spinach and toss well. Chill to serve.
Serves 4

Celery Salad

METRIC/IMPERIAL
1 head celery
Dressing:
pinch of salt
2 tablespoons soy sauce
1 tablespoon sugar
1 tablespoon sesame
  seed oil

AMERICAN
1 bunch celery
Dressing:
pinch of salt
2 tablespoons soy sauce
1 tablespoon sugar
1 tablespoon sesame
  seed oil

Discard the root and leaves of the celery. Cut the stalks into small diamond-shaped pieces by rolling each stalk half a turn every time you make a diagonal cut through. Blanch in boiling water for 1 minute. Drain and place on a serving plate.

Mix the dressing ingredients together and pour over the celery. Chill before serving.
Serves 4

Desserts

Creamy Fruit Dessert

METRIC/IMPERIAL
2 dessert apples, peeled,
  cored and thinly
  sliced
2 bananas, thinly sliced
juice of $\frac{1}{2}$ lemon
2 eggs, separated
100 g/4 oz sugar
3 tablespoons milk
3 tablespoons water
3 tablespoons cornflour

AMERICAN
2 dessert apples, peeled,
  cored and thinly
  sliced
2 bananas, thinly sliced
juice of $\frac{1}{2}$ lemon
2 eggs, separated
$\frac{1}{2}$ cup sugar
3 tablespoons milk
3 tablespoons water
3 tablespoons
  cornstarch

Arrange the apple and banana slices in alternate layers on an ovenproof dish, sprinkling each layer with lemon juice.

Put the egg yolks in a pan with the sugar, milk, water and cornflour (cornstarch). Heat very gently, stirring, until smooth, then pour over the fruit.

Beat the egg whites until stiff, then spoon over the top. Bake in a preheated hot oven (220°C/425°F, Gas Mark 7) for about 5 minutes until the top is crisp and golden. Serve hot or cold.
Serves 4

Sweet Peanut Cream

METRIC/IMPERIAL
50 g/2 oz smooth
  peanut butter
1 litre/1$\frac{3}{4}$ pints milk or
  water
4 tablespoons sugar
4 teaspoons rice flour or
  cornflour, blended
  with 4 tablespoons
  water

AMERICAN
$\frac{1}{4}$ cup smooth peanut
  butter
4$\frac{1}{4}$ cups milk or water
$\frac{1}{4}$ cup sugar
4 teaspoons rice flour or
  cornstarch, blended
  with $\frac{1}{4}$ cup water

Put the peanut butter in a saucepan and gradually stir in the milk or water to make a smooth paste. Add the sugar and bring to the boil, stirring constantly. Add the blended rice flour or cornflour (cornstarch) and cook, stirring, until the mixture thickens. Transfer to a serving bowl and serve warm.
Serves 6

Deep-Fried Sweet Potato Balls

METRIC/IMPERIAL
450 g/1 lb sweet
  potatoes
100 g/4 oz glutinous
  rice flour
50 g/2 oz brown sugar
50 g/2 oz sesame seeds
oil for deep-frying

AMERICAN
1 lb sweet potatoes
1 cup glutinous or
  sweet rice flour
$\frac{1}{3}$ cup brown sugar
$\frac{1}{2}$ cup sesame seeds
oil for deep-frying

Put the potatoes in a saucepan, cover with cold water and bring to the boil. Lower the heat and simmer for 15 to 20 minutes, or until tender. Drain and peel. Mash the potatoes, then beat in the glutinous rice flour and sugar.

With dampened hands, form the mixture into walnut-sized balls. Roll each ball in sesame seeds until well coated.

Heat the oil in a wok or deep fryer to 160°C/325°F. Deep-fry the potato balls until golden brown. Drain on kitchen paper towels. Serve hot.
Serves 4 to 6

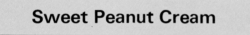

Sweet Peanut Cream (above)
Deep-Fried Sweet Potato Balls (below)

Walnut Sweet

METRIC/IMPERIAL	AMERICAN
225 g/8 oz shelled walnuts	2 cups shelled walnuts
175 g/6 oz red dates	1 cup red dates (jujubes)
oil for deep-frying	oil for deep-frying
1.75 litres/3 pints water	7½ cups water
225 g/8 oz crystal sugar or 275 g/10 oz granulated sugar	1 cup rock sugar or 1¼ cups granulated sugar
5 tablespoons cornflour, blended with 5 tablespoons water	5 tablespoons cornstarch, blended with 5 tablespoons water

Soak the walnuts in boiling water for 5 minutes, then remove the skins. Dry on kitchen paper towels.

Soak the dates in boiling water for 5 minutes, then drain and remove the stones (seeds).

Heat the oil in a wok or deep-fryer to 180°C/350°F. Deep-fry the walnuts until golden brown. (Walnuts burn easily, so remove them from the oil as soon as the colour changes.) Drain on kitchen paper towels.

Put the walnuts and dates in a blender and grind until very fine or rub through a sieve (strainer).

Bring the water to the boil in a saucepan. Stir in the sugar and walnut mixture. When the sugar has dissolved, add the blended cornflour (cornstarch) and simmer, stirring constantly, until thickened. Serve hot.
Serves 6

Caramel Apples

METRIC/IMPERIAL	AMERICAN
6 apples, peeled, cored and quartered	6 apples, peeled, cored and quartered
40 g/1½ oz plain flour	6 tablespoons all-purpose flour
1 tablespoon cornflour	1 tablespoon cornstarch
2 egg whites	2 egg whites
oil for deep-frying	oil for deep-frying
225 g/8 oz sugar	1 cup sugar
4 tablespoons water	¼ cup water
1 tablespoon sesame seeds	1 tablespoon sesame seeds

Dust the apple quarters lightly with a little of the flour. Sift the remaining flour and cornflour (cornstarch) into a bowl. Add the egg whites and mix to a smooth paste.

Heat the oil in a wok or deep-fryer to 180°C/350°F. Coat the apple quarters, one at a time, with the paste,

then drop them carefully into the oil. Fry until golden brown. Drain on kitchen paper towels.

Put the sugar and water in a small saucepan and stir until dissolved. Bring to the boil and boil until the syrup is a light golden brown. Stir in the apple quarters and sesame seeds. Transfer to lightly oiled individual serving dishes.

A bowl of cold water may be placed on the table, so that diners can pick up their apple pieces with chopsticks and lower them into the water before eating, to harden the caramel.
Serves 6

Waterchestnut Cake

METRIC/IMPERIAL	AMERICAN
150 g/5 oz waterchestnut flour	1¼ cups waterchestnut flour
350 ml/12 fl oz water	1½ cups water
450 g/1 lb canned waterchestnuts, drained and chopped	1 lb canned waterchestnuts, drained and chopped
40 g/1½ oz lard	1½ tablespoons lard
150 ml/¼ pint milk	⅔ cup milk
275 g/10 oz sugar	1¼ cups sugar

Sift the waterchestnut flour into a bowl and gradually stir in half the water. Beat to yield a smooth, soft dough.

Put the waterchestnuts, lard, milk, sugar and remaining water in a large pan. Bring to the boil, stirring. Add one third of the flour mixture and stir constantly until the mixture comes to the boil again. Remove from the heat and leave to cool for 2 minutes. Gradually add the remaining flour mixture, beating thoroughly.

Brush a deep 20 cm/8 inch square cake tin with oil. Pour in the batter. Cover the tin with a sheet of foil or greaseproof (waxed) paper and secure with string. Place the tin in a large saucepan, half-filled with water. Put on the lid and steam for 25 to 30 minutes. Leave the cake to cool in the tin.

Serve cold, cut into slices. Alternatively, to serve hot, fry the cake slices in a little oil until golden brown on both sides. Drain on kitchen paper towels and serve immediately.
Serves 4 to 6

Sweet Bean Paste Pancakes (Crêpes)

METRIC/IMPERIAL
100 g/4 oz plain flour
1 egg, beaten
150 ml/¼ pint water
6–8 tablespoons sweet
   red bean paste or
   finely chopped dates
oil for deep-frying

AMERICAN
1 cup all-purpose flour
1 egg, beaten
⅔ cup water
6–8 tablespoons sweet
   red bean sauce or
   ground dates
oil for deep-frying

Sift the flour into a large bowl, make a well in the centre and add the egg. Add the water gradually, beating constantly, to make a smooth batter.

Lightly oil an 18 cm/7 inch frying pan (skillet) and place over moderate heat. When the pan is very hot, pour in just enough batter to cover the bottom thinly, tilting the pan to spread it evenly. Cook for 30 seconds or until the underside is just firm, then carefully remove from the pan. Repeat with the remaining batter.

Divide the sweet red bean paste (sauce) or dates equally between the pancakes (crêpes), placing it in the centre of the uncooked side of each one. Fold the bottom edge over the filling, then fold the sides towards the centre, to form an envelope. Brush the edge of the top flap with a little water, fold down and press the edges together firmly to seal.

Heat the oil in a wok or deep-fryer and fry the pancakes (crêpes) for 1 minute or until crisp and golden. Remove and drain on kitchen paper towels. Serve hot.
Serves 6 to 8

Chestnut Dumplings

METRIC/IMPERIAL
1½ tablespoons dried
   yeast
2½ teaspoons sugar
3 tablespoons lukewarm
   water
450 g/1 lb plain flour
300 ml/½ pint lukewarm
   milk
1 × 225 g/8 oz can
   sweetened chestnut
   purée

AMERICAN
1½ tablespoons active
   dry yeast
2½ teaspoons sugar
3 tablespoons lukewarm
   water
4 cups all-purpose flour
1¼ cups lukewarm milk
1 × ½ lb can chestnut
   paste

Dissolve the yeast and sugar in the water. Sift the flour into a large bowl, then gradually stir in the yeast mixture and the milk. Mix to a firm dough.

Turn out onto a lightly floured surface and knead well for at least 5 minutes. Transfer to a bowl, cover with a damp cloth and leave in a warm place for 1½ to 2 hours, or until doubled in bulk.

Knead the dough on a lightly floured surface for about 5 minutes, then roll into a long 'sausage' about 5 cm/2 inches in diameter. Cut the 'sausage' into 2.5 cm/1 inch rounds. Flatten each round with the palm of the hand, then roll out until 10 cm/4 inches in diameter.

Place 1 teaspoon chestnut purée (paste) in the centre of each round, then gather up the dough around the filling to meet at the top. Twist the top of the dough to enclose the filling tightly. Leave to rest for at least 20 minutes.

Place the dumplings on a damp cloth in a steamer, leaving 2.5 cm/1 inch space between each one. Steam vigorously for 15 to 20 minutes. Serve hot.
Makes about 24

Special Chinese Ingredients

These ingredients can be bought from Chinese food stores, good delicatessens and larger supermarkets.

Bamboo shoots are the cream-coloured shoots of the bamboo plant and are crunchy in texture. Widely available canned, they should be drained before use. Also available dried — soak before using. Courgettes can be substituted for texture, but not flavour.

Bean curd, dried, is available in packets, sheets or sticks. Soak it in cold water overnight, or in warm water for one hour before use.

Bean curd, fresh, is made from puréed yellow soy beans in cakes about 7.5 cm/3 inches square and 2.5 cm/1 inch thick. It is like soft cheese in texture and as it is rather tasteless, it is used with other ingredients. It will keep fresh for several days in water in a covered container in refrigerator. There is no substitute.

Bean paste (sauce), sweet, also called red bean paste (sauce), is a thick, red soy bean paste (sauce) with sugar added. Sold in cans, it is used as a dip or as a base for sweet sauces.

Bean sauce, yellow/black is sold in cans and jars. It's a thick sauce (paste) made from crushed yellow or black soy beans mixed with flour, vinegar and spices and is often used instead of soy sauce when a thicker sauce (paste) is required in stir-frying.

Bean sprouts are the tiny crunchy shoots of mung beans. They are available fresh to be eaten on the day of purchase, or canned. They should be cooked for only a very short time to retain crispness.

Chinese cabbage (bok choy) is crunchy with a slightly sweet flavour. Can be eaten raw or cooked and is available from most good greengrocers.

Chinese dried mushrooms are available in plastic bags from Chinese food stores. They are very fragrant and will keep indefinitely in an airtight container. Soak in warm water for 20 minutes and remove the stalks. Continental dried mushrooms can be used, but ordinary mushrooms are not a good substitute.

Five-spice powder is a mixture of anise pepper, star anise, cinnamon, cloves and fennel seeds. It is strong and should be used very sparingly. It is sold in powder form or whole in a packet. Keeps indefinitely in an airtight container.

Ginger root, fresh, should be peeled before use, then sliced, crushed or shredded. To obtain the juice from the root, place the small peeled slices in a garlic crusher and squeeze firmly. Ground ginger is not an acceptable substitute but dried root ginger may be used in smaller quantities as it is sharper tasting.

Glutinous (sweet) rice flour is made from ground glutinous (sweet) rice. There is no substitute.

Hoisin sauce is a thick, brownish-red soy-based sauce with a slightly sweet, hot flavour. It can be served as a dip or used with soy sauce in stir-fried dishes. Available in cans or jars, it will keep for several months in the refrigerator.

Monosodium glutamate (msg), a chemical compound, is used to bring out the natural flavours in food. It is entirely optional in home cooking. Use sparingly — no more than $\frac{1}{4}-\frac{1}{2}$ teaspoon.

Oyster sauce is a light sauce made from oysters and soy sauce. Available in bottles, it keeps indefinitely in the refrigerator and is used for flavouring meat.

Peppercorns, Szechuan are available ground or whole for use in marinades and cooked dishes.

Sesame seed oil is a nutty-flavoured aromatic oil, generally added to dishes in a small quantity just before serving. Sold in bottles, it keeps indefinitely.

Sesame seeds are tiny and flat. They are often roasted and can be used in sweet and savoury dishes.

Soy sauce is now well-known and popular in the West. There are two varieties most commonly used. The dark sauce is stronger and thicker and imparts a rich colour to the food. It is the most suitable type to use for red-cooking. The light sauce is more delicate in flavour and is more usually used as an accompaniment or dip.

Transparent noodles are also called pea-starch or cellophane noodles. They are white and semi-transparent and should be soaked in hot water for 5 minutes before use, when they will expand. They are never eaten on their own, but are usually added to soups because they absorb some of the stock.

Water chestnuts are white, crisp and crunchy. Available ready-peeled in cans, they will keep for a month in the refrigerator. There is no substitute.

Water chestnut flour is made from water chestnuts and has a very distinctive flavour.

Wood ears are a black tree fungi and are available dried. Soak in warm water for 20 minutes before use and rinse thoroughly before and after soaking. They have very little flavour but an unusual texture; use sparingly. Available from Chinese food stores, they keep indefinitely. There is no substitute.

Index

Aubergine:
  Aubergines with
    garlic sauce 55
  Aubergine salad 55

Bean:
  Dry-cooked green
    beans 55
  Quick-fried beans in
    onion and garlic
    sauce 52
  Bean curd, Stir-fried
    bean curd with pork
    and cabbage 35
  Bean sprout salad 56
Beef:
  Beef and carrot stew 40
  Beef and egg-flower
    soup 7
  Beef and mange-tout
    44
  Braised beef with
    turnips 43
  Red-cooked beef 43
  Sautéed beef with
    mushrooms 44
  Sliced beef with
    bamboo shoot 41
  Stir-fried beef with
    broccoli 44
  Stir-fried beef with
    green peppers 41
  Stir-fried beef with
    onions 38
Braised beef with
  turnips 43
Braised chicken wings
  25
Braised fish with spring
  onions and ginger 17
Braised meatballs 33
Braised pork with
  pumpkin 43

Cabbage:
  Chinese cabbage salad
    56
  Duck and cabbage
    soup 8
  Soy-braised cabbage
    53
  Sweet and sour
    cabbage 51

Caramel apples 60
Carp with sweet and
  sour sauce 17
Cauliflower fu-yung 52
Celery salad 57
Chestnut dumplings 61
Chicken:
  Braised chicken wings
    25
  Chicken in foil 20
  Chicken and
    mushroom soup 8
  Chicken and noodle
    soup 9
  Chicken wings with
    broccoli 25
  Chicken wings stuffed
    with ham 19
  Deep-fried chicken
    with peppery hot
    sauce 19
  Diced chicken with
    brown bean sauce 28
  Diced chicken with
    celery 22
  Fried chicken legs 20
  Lemon chicken 22
  Lotus-white chicken 20
  Oil-basted chicken 21
  Pan-fried chicken
    breast 29
  Shredded chicken with
    peppers 24
  Smoked chicken 24
  Soy chicken 24
  Steamed chicken with
    Chinese mushrooms
    29
  Stewed chicken with
    chestnuts 21
  Stir-fried chicken with
    bean sprouts 21
Chinese cabbage salad
  56
Cod, Soy-braised 13
Corn soup 8
Crab omelet 11
Creamy fruit dessert 58
Crispy-skin fish 12

Deep-fried chicken with
  peppery hot sauce 19
Deep-fried meatballs 31

Deep-fried spiced fish 14
Deep-fried sweet potato
  balls 58
Diced chicken with
  brown bean sauce 28
Diced chicken with
  celery 22
Double-stir-fried pork in
  soy bean paste 38
Dry-cooked green beans
  55
Duck:
  Duck and cabbage
    soup 8
  Oil-braised duck 28
  Onion duck 28
  Peking roast duck 27
  Shredded duck salad 56

Eggplant, see Aubergine

Fish:
  Braised fish with spring
    onions and ginger 17
  Crispy-skin fish 12
  Deep-fried spiced fish 14
  Fish with bean curd in
    hot and sour sauce 16
  Fish slices in white
    sauce 13
  Red-cooked fish 13
  Steamed five willow
    fish 16
Fried chicken legs 20
Fried lamb slices with
  onions 45
Fruit, Creamy fruit
  dessert 58

Halibut, Soy-braised 13

Kidney:
  Stir-fried kidney
    flowers 48
  Sweet and sour
    kidneys 49

Lamb:
  Fried lamb slices with
    onions 45
  Red-cooked lamb 45
  Sautéed lamb with
    spring onions 35

Shredded lamb with
  noodles and spring
  onions 48
Spiced leg of lamb 45
Lemon chicken 22
Lotus-white chicken 20
Liver:
  Stir-fried liver with
    spinach 46
  Stir-fried liver with
    spring onions 49

Oil-basted chicken 21
Oil-braised duck 28
Onion duck 28

Pan-fried chicken breast
  29
Peking roast duck 27
Pickled salad 57
Pork:
  Braised meatballs 33
  Braised pork with
    pumpkin 43
  Deep-fried meatballs
    31
  Double-stir-fried pork
    in soy bean paste 38
  Pork and aubergine in
    hot sauce 46
  Pork cooked in
    barbecue sauce 40
  Pork slices with
    cauliflower 32
  Pork spareribs soup 7
  Pork and tomato soup
    7
  Red-cooked pork 36
  Shredded pork with
    bean sprouts 36
  Shredded pork and
    noodles in soup 9
  Spareribs in sweet and
    sour sauce 37
  Steamed spareribs in
    black bean sauce 32
  Stir-fried bean curd
    with pork and
    cabbage 35
  Stir-fried kidney
    flowers 48
  Stir-fried liver with
    spinach 46

Stir-fried liver with spring onions 49
Stir-fried pork with bamboo shoot 37
Sweet and sour pork 33
White-cooked boiled pork 31
Prawn:
  Prawn balls with broccoli 12
  Prawns in shells 14
  Stir-fried prawns and peas 12
  Sautéed prawns in sauce 14

Quick-fried beans in onion and garlic sauce 52
Quick-fried spinach 53

Red-cooked beef 43
Red-cooked fish 13
Red-cooked lamb 45
Red-cooked pork 36

Sautéed beef with mushrooms 44

Sautéed lamb with spring onions 35
Sautéed prawns in sauce 14
Shredded chicken with peppers 24
Shredded duck salad 56
Shredded lamb with noodles and spring onions 48
Shredded pork with bean sprouts 36
Shredded pork and noodles in soup 9
Shrimp, see Prawn
Sliced beef with bamboo shoot 41
Smoked chicken 24
Soy-braised cabbage 53
Soy-braised cod or halibut 13
Soy chicken 24
Spareribs in sweet and sour sauce 37
Spiced leg of lamb 45
Spinach:
  Quick-fried spinach 53
  Spinach salad 57

Squid, Stir-fried squid with mixed vegetables 11
Steamed chicken with Chinese mushrooms 29
Steamed five willow fish 16
Steamed spareribs in black bean sauce 32
Stewed chicken with chestnuts 21
Stir-fried bean curd with pork and cabbage 35
Stir-fried beef with broccoli 44
Stir-fried beef with green peppers 41
Stir-fried beef with onions 38
Stir-fried chicken with bean sprouts 21
Stir-fried kidney flowers 48
Stir-fried liver with spinach 46
Stir-fried liver with spring onions 49

Stir-fried mixed vegetables 51
Stir-fried pork with bamboo shoot 37
Stir-fried prawns and peas 12
Stir fried squid with mixed vegetables 11
Sweet bean paste pancakes 61
Sweet peanut cream 58
Sweet and sour cabbage 51
Sweet and sour kidneys 49
Sweet and sour pork 33

Tomato:
  Pork and tomato soup 7

Vegetables, Stir-fried mixed vegetables 51

Walnut sweet 60
Waterchestnut cake 60
White-cooked boiled pork 31

The publishers wish to acknowledge the following photographers — Paul Kemp: cover; Melvin Grey: pages 2, 15, 18, 23, 26, 30, 34, 39, 42, 50, 54, 59; Robert Golden: pages 6, 10, 47.
Illustrations by Mary Tomlin.